APPEASEMENT AND THE ROAD TO WAR

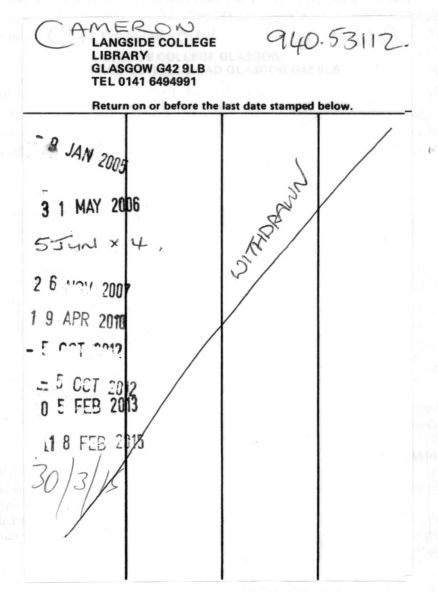

Acknowledgements

I should like to express my sincere gratitude to Mr David Cooney for invaluable help; to the Library service of Highland Regional Council, especially Mrs Mary Fleming and Ms Jenni Buskie in Tain Library, for obtaining innumerable inter-library loans; to Mrs Ellen MacKenzie and Miss Elaine Mackenzie for converting my appalling handwriting into typescript, to Mr Angus Gray for proof reading my original script, to Professor Anthony Adamthwaite for helpful comments on copyright and to Ms Liz Ottaway at the Cartoon Study Centre, University of Kent for much help with cartoon sources.

Thanks is due to Martin Secker & Warbug Ltd for permission to quote from *The Civil War in Spain 1936-39* by Robert Payne, to Harper Collins for permission to quote from *Nine Troubled Years* by Viscount Templewood; to Columbia University Press for the use of extracts from *A History of Modern Italy* by Shepard B Clough and Salvatore Saladino, to Hutchinsons for permission to use extracts from R Mannheim's translation of Hitler's *Mein Kampf*; to the *Glasgow Herald* for use of editorial material, to Rupert Hart Davies / Grafton Books for extracts from *Old Men Forget* by Duff Cooper; to Paul Hamlyn Publishing for extracts from *Hitler, a Study in Tyranny* by Alan Bullock, to the *Chigago Tribune* for extracts from Jay Allen's articles on the Spanish Civil War, to Polygon Publishing for extracts from *Voices from the Spanish Civil War* by Ian MacDougall, to Raymond Savage Ltd. for extracts from *Failure of a Mission* by Sir Neville Henderson; to Methune & Co. for extracts from A. Mayor's translation of *Ciano's Diary, 1937-38*; to MacMillan Ltd for extracts from *National Socialism in Germany* by Niall Rothnie; to Lord Lothian for permission to quote from the Lothian Papers; to Solo Syndication for permission to use extracts from *Low's Autobiography*; to HMSO for extracts from *Documents in British Foreign Policy*; to the MacMillan Company of the USA for extracts from *Mine were of Trouble* by Peter Kemp; to Longman for permission to quote from *Britain and Germany between the Wars* by Martin Gilbert and finally to the Royal Institute for International Affairs for permission to quote from *the Speeches of Adolf Hitler* by Norman H Baynes.

Permission to use photographs and cartoons was kindly given by The Centre for the Study of Cartoons and Caricature, the University of Kent at Canterbury (page 7 by Dyson, *Daily Herald* 17 May 1919; page 16 & page 45 by Lowe, *Evening Standard*; page 49 by Lowe, *Evening Standard* 20 October 1939; page 53 by Lowe in *A Cartoon History of our Times*,1939); by the Illustrated London News Picture Library (page 18 & page 43); by Popperfoto (page 24); by Hulton-Deutsch (page 47)

JRC

NF 03343l
PD 09ll99
(940.53ll2)

Published and Typeset by **Pulse Publications**
26 Burnside Gardens, Glasgow G76 7QS

Printed by **Ritchie of Edinburgh**

Graphics by Stuart McGregor

British Library Cataloguing-in-Publication Data
A Catalogue record for this book is
available from the British Library

ISBN 0 948766 10 7

© Ronald Cameron 1991

Reprinted 1994

Contents

TIMECHART

1919

18 January: Versailles Peace Conference began.
14 February: Covenant of League of Nations approved.
28 June: Treaty of Versailles signed.

1920

19 March: US Senate finally rejects Versailles Treaty and League.

1921

25 August: US and Germany sign separate peace treaty in Berlin.

1923

11 January: Franco-Belgian invasion of the Ruhr starts.

1925

27 August: Last French troops withdrawn from Ruhr.
16 October: Treaty of Mutual Guarantee (Locarno, Switzerland).

1926

10 September: Germany admitted to League.

1928

27 August: Kellogg-Briand Pact (Pact of Paris).

1929

24 October: Wall St Crash. Start of Great Depression.

1931

23 August: British Labour Cabinet split on Sterling Crisis and spending cuts.
24 August: MacDonald resigns as Labour Prime Minister, becomes Prime Minister of National Government.
18 September: Mukden Incident.

1932

28 January: Japanese attack Shanghai.
2 February: Disarmament Conference opens at Geneva.
3 February: Lytton Commission leaves for Manchuria.
9 March: Japanese proclaim independent state of Manchukuo.
11 March: League refuses to recognise Manchukuo.

1933

30 January: Hitler Chancellor of Germany.
24 February: League adopts Lytton Report on Manchuria.
27 March: Japan withdraws from League.
14 October: Germany leaves Geneva Disarmament Conference. Announces intention to leave League.

1934

26 January: Hitler makes non-aggression pact with Poland.
25 July: Attempted Nazi 'Putsch' in Austria fails.
18 September: USSR admitted to League.
5 December: Wal Wal incident (Abyssinia).

1935

13 January: Plebiscite, Saar votes to return to Germany.
16 March: Conscription announced in Germany. Existence of Luftwaffe admitted.
14 April: Stresa Front. France, Italy, Britain.
2 May : Franco-Soviet Pact.
16 May: Czech-Soviet Pact.
7 June: Baldwin replaces MacDonald as Prime Minister of Britain.
18 June: Anglo-German Naval Agreement.
3 October: Italian invasion of Abyssinia.
8 December: Hoare-Laval Plan revealed.

1936

16 February: Popular Front Government takes office in Spain.
7 March: Hitler renounces Locarno Pacts. Remilitarises Rhineland.
5 May: Italians capture Addis Ababa. Abyssinia annexed by Italy.
11 July: Austro-German agreement.
17 July: Spanish Civil War starts.
2 August: Non-intervention suggested by French
1 November: Rome-Berlin Axis.
25 November: Anti-Comintern Pact (Japan and Germany).

1937

11 February: Battle of Jarama. Nationalist assault of Madrid held.
8 March: Battle of Guadalajara. Italian Fascists beaten back by Republicans and International Brigades. Madrid 'saved'.
26 April: Guernica destroyed by German Condor Legion bombers.
31 May: Neville Chamberlain becomes Prime Minister of Britain.
10 June: Fall of Bilbao (Basque capital) to Franco.
14 September: Nyon Agreement in Non-Intervention Committee.
23 September: Mussolini's visit to Germany.
6 November: Italy joins Anti-Comintern Pact.
11 December: Italy withdraws from League.
15 December: Republicans capture Teruel from Nationalists.

1938

23 February: Teruel captured by Nationalists.
2 March: Hitler visits Italy.
13 March: Austrian Anschluss.
16 March: Britain recognises Italian regime in Abyssinia.
28 March: Konrad Henlein visits Hitler.
24 April: Henlein's Karlsbad Speech. The eight demands.
20 May: Czech army mobilised against rumours of German troop movements. May Crisis; Britain, France and Russia warn off Hitler.
15 September: Chamberlain meets Hitler at Berchtesgaden Berghof.
22 September: International Brigades sent home by Republican Government in the hope that the League would get Germany and Italy to withdraw from Spain.
22-23 September: Chamberlain and Hitler meet at Bad Godesberg.
28 September: 'Black Wednesday'. Europe preparing for war. French put new plan. Mussolini proposes Conference.
29-30 September: Munich conference and agreement.
1 October: German troops enter Sudetenland. Poland takes Teschen, Hungary takes South Slovakia.
24 October: Germans raise the return of Danzig with the Poles.

1939

26 January: Barcelona falls to Spanish Nationalists.
15 March: Germans sieze Bohemia and Moravia.
23 March: Lithuania obliged to cede Memel to Germany.
30 March: Franco's troops enter Madrid. End of Spanish Civil War.
31 March: Britain and France issue guarantees to Poland.
7 April: Italian invasion of Albania.
16 April: British and French open talks about Poland with Russians.
28 April: Hitler renounces German-Polish Non-Aggression Pact and Anglo-German Naval Agreement.
22 May: Hitler and Mussolini conclude Pact of Steel.
12 August: British and French try to revive talks with Russians.
23 August: Nazi-Soviet Non-Aggression Pact signed.
1 September: German invasion of Poland.
3 September: Britain and France declare war against Germany.

WHO'S WHO ?

Stanley Baldwin (1867-1947): Conservative MP 1908-37. Prime Minister 1923-24, 1924-29, 1935-37.

Josef Beck, Colonel (1894-1944): Polish Foreign Minister 1932-39.

Eduard Benes (1884-1948): Czech representative at Versailles. Foreign Minister 1918-35. President 1935-38. Led Czech government in exile in London during Second World War. Returned to Prague after war.

Leon Blum (1872-1950): Leader of French Socialist Party. Prime Minister of Popular Front Governments 1936-37 and 1938. Imprisoned by Germans. Prime Minister 1946-47.

Neville Chamberlain (1869-1940): (Son of Joseph Chamberlain, Cabinet Minister and Liberal Imperialist.) Neville Chamberlain managed sisal plantation in Bahamas 1890-97. Lord Mayor Birmingham 1915-16. Conservative MP 1918-40. Chancellor of Exchequer 1923-24 and 1931-37. Prime Minister 1937-40. Followed policy of appeasement towards Hitler.

Winston Churchill (1864-1965): (Son of Conservative Cabinet Minister, Lord Randolph Churchill). He served in the British army in the Sudan and covered Boer War 1900-02 as a journalist. Elected to Parliament as a Liberal. Supported Lloyd George in introduction of social reforms. First Lord of the Admiralty 1911-15 and again 1939-40, having crossed the House to join Conservatives after First World War. Chancellor of the Exchequer 1926-29. Advocate of rearmament and opponent of appeasement in the 30s. Prime Minister 1940-45 and 1951-55.

Francisco Franco (1892-1975): Joined Spanish army as an officer cadet aged 14. Fought Riffs in Morocco. Severely wounded 1916. Youngest general in army. Did not join Monarchist revolt in 1932. Assumed command of Army revolt against Popular Front Government after the accidental death of General Sanjurjo. Declared to be 'Chief of the Spanish State' ('Il Caudillo') in 1936 at start of rising. Ruled Spain from the defeat of the Republic until his death.

Count Galleazzo Ciano: Married to Mussolini's daughter, Eda. Mussolini's Foreign Minister. Turned against Mussolini in later stages of World War Two. Executed by fascists in Verona jail 1944.

Herman Göring (1893-1946): World War One air ace. Leading Nazi. Participated in Putsch of 1923. Air Minister and Commander in Chief German Airforce 1933-45. Held other important offices. Committed suicide after being condemned to death as a war criminal.

Anthony Eden (1897-1977): Fought in World War One. Conservative MP 1923-57. Minister for League of Nations Affairs 1935-38. Foreign Secretary 1935-38. Became increasingly opposed to appeasement. Prime Minister 1955-57.

Lord Halifax (1881-1959): Conservative MP 1910-25. Foreign Secretary 1938-40. Advocate of appeasement.

Neville Henderson (1882-1942): Diplomat. A___ to Berlin 1937-39. Encouraged Chamberlain to t___

Adolf Hitler (1889-1945): Served in World W___ Wounded and gassed. Awarded Iron Cross (1st ___ Founder and leader of Nazi Party. Chancellor of Germ___ 1933-45.

Samuel Hoare (1880-1959): Conservative MP 1910-44. Held various cabinet offices including Foreign Secretary 1935. Responsible for Hoare-Laval Pact on Abyssinia. Made Viscount Templewood in 1944.

Pierre Laval (1883-1946): Socialist and virtual pacifist. French Prime Minister 1931-32. Foreign Minister 1934-35. Responsible for Hoare-Laval Pact on Abyssinia. Prime Minister 1935-36. Collaborated with Germans during occupation by setting up puppet Vichy regime. Executed as traitor 1946.

J Ramsay MacDonald (1866-1937): Labour MP 1906-18 and 1922-37. Prime Minister and Foreign Secretary 1924. Prime Minister 1929-32 (Labour) and 1932-37 (National Government).

Benito Mussolini (1883-1945): Journalist and rabble rouser. Founded Italian Fascist Party. President council of Ministers 1922-26. Prime Minister 1926-43. Executed by Italian Partisans 28 April 1945.

Ras Tafari Makonnen otherwise the **Emperor Haile Selassie I** (1892-1975): (Son of the Emperor Menelik's cousin.) Regent 1916. Crowned Emperor 1930. Driven into exile by Italians 1936. Restored by British during World War Two. Deposed in Marxist military coup 1974. Died in captivity of 'circulatory failure'.

Joachim von Ribbentrop (1893-1946): German Ambassador to London 1936-38. Nazi Foreign Minister 1938-45. Executed as war criminal 1946.

Joseph Stalin (1879-1953): From state of Georgia. Joined Social Democratic Party (Marxist) 1898. Founded *Pravda* 1911. Involved in revolution of October 1917. Elected General Secretary of Central Committee of the Communist Party of the Soviet Union 1922. Signed non-aggression pact with Nazi Germany, August 1939. Marshall of the Soviet Union 1943. Generalissimo 1943.

Gustav Stresemann (1878-1929): Chancellor of Germany 1923, thereafter Foreign Minister. Sought non-violent revision of Versailles Treaty and the establishment of friendly relations with Britain and France.

Jan Christiaan Smuts (1870-1950): Boer General. British Field Marshall. Fought in World War One. One of two South African Commissioners at Versailles Conference. Criticised Treaty as being too harsh on Germany. Prime Minister of South Africa 1919-29 and 1939-48.

Robert Vansittart (1881-1957): Civil Servant. Permanent Under Secretary at Foreign Office 1930-38. Chief diplomatic Adviser to Foreign Secretary 1938-41. Increasingly uneasy about appeasement. Saw need for rearmament.

1 THE LEAGUE OF NATIONS

COLLECTIVE SECURITY AND APPEASEMENT

"The road to hell is paved with good intentions."

After four years of purgatory in the First World War there was an almost universal desire for lasting peace. Statesmen in and beyond Europe strove to establish a system which would preserve peace or at least prevent war. Despite their efforts the world was again plunged into bloodshed in 1939. This book attempts to explain why this happened and why good intentions are not always enough.

Woodrow Wilson, prophet of democracy, President of the USA and America's chief representative at the Versailles Conference, was mainly responsible for the idea of *collective security*. He said, "... it is our duty to maintain the safeguards which will see to it that the mothers of America and the mothers of France and England and Italy and Belgium and all the other suffering nations should never be called upon for this sacrifice again. This can be done. It must be done and it will be done. The great thing that these men left us is... the great instrument of the *League of Nations*."

Wilson maintained that peace could be preserved by the nations of the world acting together to control any aggression and settle disputes. The League of Nations, his great gift to humanity, was to be the main agency of collective security. It was established at the Versailles Conference and each of the defeated nations was required to sign its Charter, almost as a guarantee of future good behaviour. Forty two nations joined the League immediately, but this privilege was denied to the defeated powers and Russia. The League was also seriously weakened by Wilson's failure to persuade the American Congress to ratify America's membership. Thus, at the outset, the whole idea of collective security was drastically undermined by the failure of the world's greatest power to join and support it.

Appeasement

Collective security was not the only idea for preserving peace current in the twenties and thirties. A growing number of political leaders and opinion shapers, especially in Britain and the USA, came to favour an attitude of mind they called *appeasement*. Professor Keith Robbins of Glasgow University has defined it as " a disposition to avoid conflict by judicious concession and negotiation". Robbins pointed out that the difficulty lies in deciding when concessions are well-judged and reasonable and what these concessions should be.

Collective security and appeasement do not need to be contradictory policies. Making reasonable concessions to a country with genuine grievances may help to secure peace and strengthen collective security. If, on the other hand, concessions are made at the expense of small nations in an attempt to buy off larger and more aggressive powers,

collective security has clearly ceased to function. This is what appeared to happen in the thirties when Japan, Germany and Italy demanded more territory.

Despite its association with the thirties, appeasement was not a new strategy then, and it has continued to be used, sometimes with success, in more recent times. In the interwar years its use by the British government stemmed from a variety of factors, the most important of which were:

1 The belief that Germany and Italy had been mistreated in the peace settlement of 1919 and that concessions had to be granted to correct decisions made in anger and bitterness at the end of a long and destructive war. Few French statesmen felt this way about Germany.

2 The belief that the people of Britain and the Empire were weary of war and would not accept another, even in support of collective security.

3 The belief that the British economy had been too severely damaged by the Great War and the Great Depression to sustain another major war.

4 The belief that the armed forces of Britain and France were neither prepared nor equipped for war in the thirties and needed time to rearm.

These factors are examined in detail later in this book.

PEACE AND FUTURE CANNON FODDER

(A prophetic cartoon- Clemenceu leaving the conference, which had met to ensure peace, hears one of the children it had doomed to be a soldier in 1940 weeping at his fate.)

Organisation of the League of Nations

The League had its headquarters at Geneva in neutral Switzerland. The *Assembly* was its parliament in which all member nations had one vote. It debated important issues, controlled the budget and vetted new members, but it was not in permanent session.

Day-to-day decision making was left to the *Council* which in 1930 had five permanent members: Britain, France, Italy, Japan and Germany (admitted in 1926). The Council always contained a number of temporary members elected by the Assembly.

A *Secretariat* existed to record the decisions of the Assembly and Council and to carry out various administrative duties.

The Permanent Court of International Justice w as located in the Hague in Holland. Its judges would give decisions if requested to do so by both parties to a dispute. They also gave advice to the Assembly and Council on matters relating to international law and treaties.

The *Covenant of the League* not only described its organisation, it also embodied a logical system of measures for settling international disputes and containing aggression.

ARTICLE 10 bound the member states to protect and preserve the territorial integrity and political independence of all other member states.

ARTICLE 11 stated that any war, or threat of war, was the League's concern, even if it did not involve members, and that the League could take any action it deemed suitable to preserve peace. It also gave any member the right to draw the attention of the League to any problem which threatened peace.

ARTICLES 12 and 15 described the various ways in which the League might peacefully resolve disputes between nations.

ARTICLE 16 described the sanctions which might be applied against a nation which attacked a member. If it failed to respond to moral condemnation, economic sanctions could be used. Members would cease to trade with or lend money to the aggressor. More serious and sustained cases could lead to military sanctions with member states being called on to contribute military, naval or air forces for armed action against the culprit. Aggressors could also be expelled from the League.

Reaction to the League

Despite the popular enthusiasm for it at the outset, most of the world's leading statesmen had grave misgivings about the League.

French statesmen felt that the League wasn't strong enough and lacked the means to police its decisions. They were fearful of the possibility of German rearmament and were unwilling to disarm themselves until they were certain that a peaceful German democratic republic had been firmly established and that German militarism was finally dead.

In Britain there were those who feared that the League might require them to apply economic or military sanctions in a cause which they regarded as unjust. The passage of time proved to the British that the League was most unlikely to force them to take any such action and by the thirties British leaders were happy to say that the League was "the cornerstone of British Foreign Policy". This claim, however, is a debatable one - made by the National Government in the run-up to the 1935 General Election in order to win wide electoral support.

Mussolini's assumption of power in Italy radically affected Italian attitudes. The purpose of the League was to keep the peace, while Fascism was a philosophy which glorified war and conquest. (Demonstrated by Mussolini's claim that, "A day on the battlefield is worth a thousand years of peace !") The Fascists saw that the League could act as a brake on Italy's expansionist aims. It suited Britain and France who already had all the colonies they wanted, but its actions could only serve to keep Italy poor.

The USSR was initially very hostile to the League, seeing it as an anti-Soviet organisation which would enable the "Imperialist Powers", Britain and France, to dominate smaller nations. Gradually this hostility mellowed until, finally, the USSR joined the League in 1934.

The USA had, by its refusal to join the League, retreated into isolation. American leaders, such as Herbert Hoover who was President from 1928 to 1932, tended to regard the League as "something for the European Nations" but unnecessary in the western hemisphere where 'Uncle Sam' was perfectly capable of looking after things. Most Americans did not want to become too closely involved with the League in case they were dragged into another European war.

Germany looked to the League to oblige the powers which had defeated her in the Great War to disarm, following the lead which she had been forced to take. If this failed, Germany believed she should be permitted to rearm. Germany, like Italy, was a 'revisionist' power in her attitude to the Treaty of Versailles. The Germans felt deeply aggrieved by their treatment in 1919. Whether they were justified in feeling this way is largely irrelevant. When Hitler, with his brand of aggressive, expansionist Nationalism, came to power in 1933, their calls for changes to the Treaty made huge demands on the mechanism of Collective Security. British leaders, in particular, came to feel that the League was incapable of dealing with the situation and that they should negotiate directly with the revisionist states to effect their appeasement and preserve peace.

The League in Action - 1919 to 1931

The years 1920 to 1931 are sometimes called the 'Golden Years of the League of Nations'. During this period, it had a number of successes in settling disputes between minor powers and also distinguished itself in humanitarian work. However, even in these halcyon days of the League there were ominous pointers to the future in two or three disputes. In these, great powers deliberately by-passed the machinery of the League and haggled among

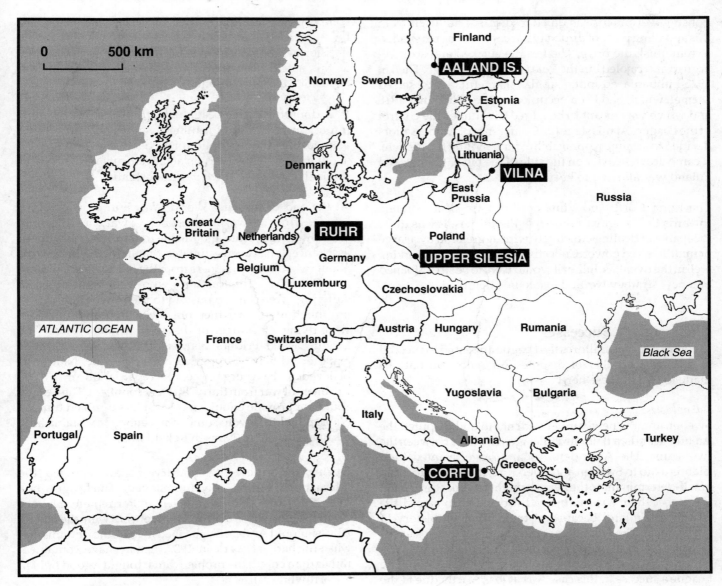

Europe in 1923 and some cases for the league

themselves to sort out a compromise which suited them, but which was not the result of the principled, judicial and court-like procedure that the League sought to establish.

The Ruhr, 1923

The first real challenge to the League was the Franco-Belgian invasion of the Ruhr in 1923. The pretext for this invasion was that Germany had fallen behind with her reparations payments, but to nations that had been neutral in the Great War it looked like a piece of old-fashioned, naked aggression. The Swedes intended to raise the matter with the League but abandoned this plan when the French made it clear that they would leave the League before they would withdraw from the Ruhr.

Corfu, 1923

The next of these problems arose when Mussolini ordered the invasion of the Greek island of Corfu in 1923, following the murder of an Italian general who had been part of an international boundary commission attempting to define the frontier between Greece and Albania. There was no real evidence that the Greeks were to blame, but the Italians bombarded and then occupied Corfu, rejected a League of Nations report and refused to leave until the Conference of Ambassadors (a body which had developed

from the Versailles Peace Conference and whose task was to supervise the new territorial arrangements) had ordered the Greeks to pay compensation. This was not the way in which the League had intended to resolve disputes. It was a clear case of 'might is right' and bore no resemblance to impartial legal justice. The fact that the League could so easily be brushed aside when a major power was the aggressor was a bad omen. It was clear that the greater powers in the League would not take on a powerful nation simply to obtain justice for a small one.

Vilna: Poland v Lithuania

A dispute between Poland and Lithuania over the city of Vilna had smouldered on and on since 1918. Both countries wanted it. Most of the people in the city were Jews, but there was also a substantial Polish population and an ancient Polish University. The people of the surrounding countryside were Lithuanians and Russians. When Lithuania became independent from Russia in 1918, she claimed Vilna as her capital, a claim recognised by the Soviets in 1920. The Poles tried to take it by force but, to the surprise of the world's military experts, they failed. An armistice was signed which left the Lithuanians in control. Then, acting on his own initiative, a Polish General suddenly seized the city, taking the Lithuanians by surprise. The

9

Polish government was quick to disassociate itself from this appalling piece of duplicity but could not be persuaded to relinquish the prize. The League clucked and scolded, argued and cajoled but the Poles would not budge. Then in 1923 Lithuania, adopting similar shameful tactics, seized Memel, which had been occupied by the allies since 1918 and which was meant to be a Free City under the control of the League. At this stage the Conference of Ambassadors decided to assume responsibility for handling the dispute. It came down heavily on the side of the big battalions and Poland was allowed to keep Vilna.

The Ruhr, Corfu and Vilna episodes are clear pointers towards the League's failures in the thirties. It was quite incapable of dealing effectively with aggression by a large or middle-sized power. Collective security was not working well in the twenties. Either it would have to be strengthened or a new strategy would have to be attempted.

The League's Successes

In contrast to these failures the League appeared to succeed in settling a number of disputes. Reference can only be made to two of these here.

Aaland Isles

Sweden and the newly independent Finland disputed the Aaland Islands, a Baltic archipelago which lay between the two states. The Aalanders, by and large, wanted their islands to go to Sweden and, therefore, under the doctrine of self-determination, the League might have been expected to respect their wishes. Instead it decided to award the islands to Finland because of their previous history of government. The Aalanders were to be granted a substantial measure of local self-government and their rights as a minority people would be protected by the League. The League's success in this case was at least partly due to the attitude of the high-minded Swedes who were keen for the League to succeed and willing to make sacrifices to that end.

Silesia

After the Treaty of Versailles, the people who lived in the various territories which were to be detached from Germany were given the chance to make their feelings known in plebiscites organised by the victorious powers. In some areas, such as Schleswig-Holstein, the results were clear cut and easy to act on. Upper Silesia proved to be a problem. The victors intended that this coal and iron rich area should become part of Poland. The Germans claimed, quite rightly, that this had always been a German area and that its Polish population had migrated in to work in the mines and industries which the Germans had established. The plebiscite showed 60% of the population wanted to remain under German rule, the rest favoured Poland. The victors intended to transfer those districts with a Polish majority to Poland and allow Germany to retain the rest. The French Commissioners wanted to hand over a very large part of the territory, while the British and Italians intended to be more generous to Germany. The dispute became more and more acrimonious until somebody suggested that the League should be asked to take it on. Showing neither imagination nor courage, the League suggested a compromise between the Anglo-Italian and the somewhat outrageous French proposals. This compromise was implemented. Since the French view had been regarded as absurdly biased towards the Poles, this decision helped to turn German opinion against the League at this stage. Elsewhere the settlement of the Silesian problem was hailed as a major triumph for the League.

It is doubtful if the League's performance in its most important role, that of settling disputes and preventing wars, justifies the description of the twenties as the League's 'Golden Age'. However, its achievements in the field of humanitarian work were more substantial.

At the end of the First World War, Europe was full of refugees from the war and prisoners of war, most of whom were utterly destitute and unable to return home without assistance. It has been estimated that in Russia there were about two million prisoners from the old Austrian Empire and Germany. The Russians, who were accustomed to suffering, were far too busy with their own problems to pay much attention to their prisoners, thousands of whom were dying of hunger or diseases such as typhus. The League asked Fridtjof Nansen, the Norwegian Arctic explorer, to help. Supported by the League, Nansen is believed to have organised the repatriation of 400,000 prisoners of war from thirty different countries. The League could not provide enough money at this troubled time, so Nansen had to devote some of his energy to establishing his own charitable 'Nansen Relief Fund'.

During the nineteenth century, Britain had led the international campaign against slavery. The League took over this role and established a Permanent Slavery Commission, whose main areas of concern were the Sudan, Abyssinia and Arabia. Established in 1924, the Commission was still hard at work in 1937. It may have contained, rather than cured, the problem but it fought a good fight in a worthwhile cause.

An equally difficult problem to deal with was the international trade in narcotics and dangerous drugs. The League investigated the trade and attempted to educate people about the dangers of drug abuse. It tried to get its members to work together to restrict the traffic but success was limited. As modern operatives in this field would understand, it was a difficult and unrewarding task - a constant struggle against misplaced human ingenuity. At least they tried.

France's Search for Security

International relations remained poor for several years after the Treaty of Versailles. The French did not regard the settlement and the League as an adequate guarantee of their security and the Russian Revolution had denied them their main prewar ally. In 1920 they concluded a military alliance with Belgium and then they made a series of alliances with the new small nations of Eastern Europe - with Poland (1921), Czechoslovakia (1924), Rumania (1926) and Yugoslavia (1927). This system of alliances, known as the Little Entente, did not give France the security she craved since even the aggregate power of these nations did not match the loss of Russia. It also marked a departure from the ideal of collective security and a drift back to the bad old habit of power block politics which was held to be one of the major causes of the First World War.

The Germans were quick to sense what was happening and felt threatened by encirclement. Germany and Russia, the two 'leper nations' of Europe, both excluded from the League, began to draw together. In 1922, Lloyd George organised a conference at Genoa to discuss arrangements for Russia to pay interest on some of her prewar debts. The Russians were totally unco-operative with the allies but at nearby Rapallo they concluded an agreement with the Germans , most of the details of which were secret. By this time, the Germans were actively evading the disarmament clauses of the Treaty of Versailles. At Rapallo it was agreed that they would make an annual payment to the Russians and, in return, selected German officers would go to Russia to be trained in the use of tanks, heavy artillery and military aircraft, all of which Germany was forbidden to possess. This arrangement continued until 1935 when German rearmament had gone so far that it was no longer useful or necessary.

Suspicion about the true nature of the Rapallo agreement alarmed the French so much that it became the real reason for their disastrous invasion of the Ruhr in 1923 which marked the low point in international relations in the 1920s.

During the twenties the French made a number of proposals designed to strengthen the League so that it could act speedily in their defence should they be attacked again by Germany. These came to nothing as they were rejected by Britain and other countries who suspected that the French might try to involve them in unnecessary wars against Germany.

Building Bridges, 1924 to 1929

The Locarno Agreement, 1925

After the Ruhr fiasco, the anti-German Raymond Poincaré was replaced as Foreign Minister of France by the more conciliatory Aristide Briand, while Gustav Stresemann became Germany's Foreign Minister. Stresemann was willing to try to fulfill the terms of Versailles - if only to prove that they were unworkable. This applied especially to reparations. He sought progress through conciliation. His attitude and that of Briand enabled the Dawes Plan of 1924 to relax the reparations arrangements. As a result collective security was strengthened again in 1925 when Britain, Germany, France and Italy signed a *Treaty of Mutual Guarantee* at Locarno in Switzerland. Germany accepted and guaranteed her frontiers with France and Belgium, although she was still unwilling to accept her eastern frontiers as a final arrangement. The British Foreign Secretary, Sir Austen Chamberlain, said in the House of Commons,

> "...the agreements made at Locarno, valuable as they are in themselves ... are yet more valuable for the spirit which produced them... We regard Locarno, not as the end of the work of appeasement, but as its beginning... I had not met the representatives of the German Empire until I met them at the Conference. I very soon was able to satisfy myself that they came there animated by the same desire for peace and reconciliation that animated the Western Nations."
> (*Hansard* , quoted by Martin Gilbert in *Britain and Germany between the Wars*)

In this case most of the concessions were being made by the Germans, who might therefore be said to be appeasing France. Sir Austen clearly meant to say the German Republic and not the German Empire. This is one of the earliest uses of the word 'appeasement' by a British politician in the context of international relations in this era.

The Kellogg-Briand Pact, 1928

Collective security reached a new high point when the American Secretary of State, Kellogg, and Aristide Briand drew up the Pact of Paris, otherwise known as the Kellogg-Briand Pact or the Treaty Renouncing War, by which 62 nations promised not to use war as a means of resolving disputes - unless in self-defence.

Further evidence of the improved climate in international affairs can be seen when Germany, with the approval of Briand, was admitted to the League as a Council member in 1926. The reconciliation which Briand and Stresemann initiated might have given Europe peace if it had been given time to develop but the death of Stresemann in 1929, the Great Depression (1929-1935) and the consequent rise to power of Adolf Hitler meant that this was not to be.

DISARMAMENT 1919-1934

Article 8 of the Covenant of the League of Nations demanded that "national armaments" be reduced "to the lowest point consistent with national safety...". In the twenties statesmen were very involved with ideas of security. The British and Americans were convinced that the arms race had been a major cause of the First World War and that disarmament would provide security against further wars. France, whose experiences in 1870 and 1914 had made her realise the need for strong defences, was much more concerned with security against defeat and frequently obstructed plans for disarmament. While the British and Americans blythly assumed that peace would follow disarmament, the French took the attitude that disarmament could only follow guaranteed peace. The dispute is remarkably similar to the debate between the unilateral and multilateral disarmers of the nuclear age.

In November 1920 the League appointed a 'Temporary Mixed Commission' to draw up proposals for disarmament, but in the normal traditions of the League, things did not happen quickly. In 1922 the Commission rejected British proposals to impose limitations on land forces. Nothing happened after that for several years and the Temporary Mixed Commission lapsed.

In 1925 the League Council set up a Commission to prepare for an International Disarmament Conference. The USA participated although it was not in the League. It soon became obvious that, although the great powers agreed to disarmament in principle, they would not agree to any detailed proposals. As a consequence, the Conference being prepared by the Commission did not take place until February 1932, and when it did, the great powers were still nowhere near to a consensus on how disarmament could be achieved.

When the Disarmament Conference was finally convened in Geneva in 1932 sixty six countries were represented, five of whom were not members of the League. The Chairman was Arthur Henderson, appointed in 1931 while Foreign Secretary in Britain's Labour Government. In the intervening period he had resigned his post and then lost his seat in Parliament in the 1931 General Election. It did not help the Conference to have a chairman who represented nobody but himself.

As the delegates gathered the Japanese were busy with their conquest of Manchuria, a fact that did not enhance enthusiasm for disarming. The Preparatory Commission had failed to provide an agenda of promising ideas to pursue but at least if had highlighted the problems which would be encountered.

In July 1932, just before the summer recess, the Conference voted to:
- ban aerial bombing and to control civil aviation.
- limit the numbers of heavy tanks and guns although they had yet to agree on what they meant by heavy.
- ban chemical warfare, but not the manufacture or possession of chemical weapons.

Only Germany and the USSR voted against these proposals. The Germans said that they would not return to the Conference until the other countries agreed to reduce their armaments to Germany's level or allowed Germany to re-arm to theirs. In a speech at this time Hitler said,

"Germany has disarmed. She has complied with all obligations imposed on her in the Peace Treaty to an extent far beyond the limits of equity and reason... Germany has thus a fully justified moral claim to the fulfilment by the other Powers of their obligations under the Treaty of Versailles... Has not Germany , in her state of defencelessness and disarmament, greater justification in demanding security than the over-armed States bound together in military alliances ?"
"Nevertheless Germany is at any time willing to undertake further obligations..., if all the other nations are ready ... to do the same... Germany would also be perfectly ready to disband her entire military establishment and destroy the small amount of arms remaining to her, if the neighbouring countries will do the same thing with equal thoroughness..."
(*Speeches of Adolf Hitler* edited by Norman Baynes pp 1052-1053)

When the Conference reconvened in the autumn the Germans were absent and were only tempted back two months later when offered a guarantee of "equality of rights in a system which would provide security for all nations". In order to placate the Germans the French did actually cut their arms spending in 1932 -33. Their deep concern for 'security' was in no way reduced by German demands, made in January 1933, that they disarm still further.

In March 1933 Ramsay MacDonald, the British Prime Minister, presented Conference with a detailed plan which quantified the armed forces permitted to every country in Europe. The Germans were also guaranteed equality of armaments within five years. The plan was welcomed at first but arguments soon broke out over the figures and in the end nothing came of it.

That summer produced a French suggestion that four years should be spent on setting up an international agency to supervise armament levels. Arms reductions could begin during a second four year period. This was not enough for the new German government under ex-corporal Hitler. When the British and Italians accepted the French plan in October 1933, the Germans withdrew from the Disarmament Conference and the League.

For the next six months the great powers exchanged notes. In February 1934, Hitler offered to limit the German army to any size which would be applied equally to the French, Polish and Italian armies and to accept quota style restrictions on his airforce. The French did not trust Hitler to keep his word and demanded extra guarantees. Finally they refused to discuss the offer on the grounds that Hitler had every intention of rearming anyway. Although the Disarmament Conference continued to hold occasional sessions until the end of the year and was never formally wound up, it was, to all intents an purposes, finished after February 1934. A new arms race had begun and some of the runners were quicker off the mark than others.

Collective action had failed to solve the problem of armaments levels. It is hardly surprising that statesmen concerned to preserve peace should have wanted to try another approach. This led to British attempts to appease Germany.

THE MANCHURIAN CRISIS
Most people in Britain would blame Hitler, or perhaps the Germans, for starting the Second World War, but before he came to power the Japanese had already shown the limitations of the system designed to keep the peace.

After their war with Russia in 1904, they took over the lease on Russia's railway through Manchuria, a province of China.

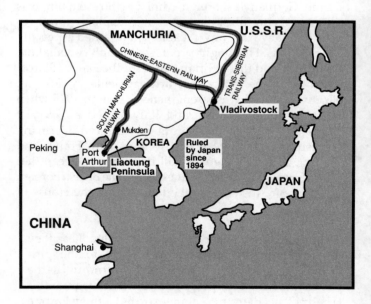

Japan's relations with China deteriorated steadily from the time of the Great War. At home their liberal-democratic government was seriously threatened by the rise of aggressive, neo-Fascist, nationalism, especially in the army. This was due in part to economic difficulties and also to a

feeling that they were being treated as a second-rate power and inferior people by the Americans. Japanese Nationalists saw expansion in Manchuria as a solution to both of these problems.

One night in September 1931 an explosion occurred which did minor damage to the Japanese South Manchurian Railway at Mukden. It is impossible to say who was responsible. The Japanese blamed the Chinese but there is evidence that they may have sabotaged the track themselves to excuse their subsequent actions. Japanese troops poured out of the railway zone and took over all the important towns in Manchuria in a three day operation which was a model of military planning and co-ordination. By early January the army had taken over the entire province. It was clearly acting on its own initiative and had successfully resisted attempts by the Tokyo government to bring it under control and end the invasion.

In February they announced that Manchuria had become the independent Republic of Manchukuo.

Soon after the Mukden incident the Chinese had taken their case to the League of Nations. Unanimous agreement was reached on the call to send a League Commission to China to investigate the problem. It set sail in February 1932, six months after the dispute began, and was chaired by the British representative, Lord Lytton. The USA, France, Germany and Italy were also represented.

Lord Lytton's report did not become available to the League until September 1932, a year after the Mukden incident. It contained a long and detailed study, not only of recent incidents but also of the history of China's relations with Japan. While it accepted that Japan had indeed been provoked, it rejected the notion that she had acted in self-defence and had merely carried out a police action. It also dismissed the Japanese claim that 'Manchukuo' was a fully independent state rather than a puppet regime wholly dependent on the Japanese army .

Lytton said that a return to the old situation in Manchuria would not work and that the Chinese and Japanese should negotiate, with help from the League, to establish an independent state in Manchuria. This did not appeal to the Japanese who feared the loss of their investments, or to the Chinese who did not want to lose what they considered to be their territory. The League considered Lytton's recommendations and then issued a report which followed them almost exactly.

The great powers were unwilling to consider sanctions against Japan because of economic problems at home, the practical difficulties of waging war a long way from home and because of American reluctance to be involved.

On 17th February 1933 Winston Churchill spoke on Manchuria in the House of Commons:

"Now I must say something to you which is very unfashionable. I am going to say a word of sympathy for Japan, not necessarily for her policy , but for her position and her national difficulties. I do not think the League of Nations would be well-advised to quarrel with Japan. The League has great work to do in Europe... there is no more use affronting Japan than there would be in ordering the Swiss and Czechoslovak navies to the Yellow Sea... I hope we in England shall try to understand a little the position of Japan, an ancient State, with the highest sense of national honour and patriotism, and with a teeming population and a remarkable energy. On the one side they see the dark menace of Soviet Russia. On the other the chaos of China..."

Churchill, the backbench maverick, had said what many in power had been thinking.

In February 1933 the report was formally adopted by the League. The Japanese delegation walked out and a month later Japan withdrew from the League. Their regime in Manchukuo was not recognised but they had got away with aggression and showed that a strong power could attack a weak one without fear of the League which was now seen to be two war-weary old powers, Britain and France, rather than as a dynamic combination of greater and lesser nations, ready and willing to act to preserve peace. The League had been shown to be very slow to act and willing to go to any length to avoid applying sanctions of any sort. These were lessons that others would not be slow to learn. However, despite this setback, the League was still considered to be potentially useful in Europe where it carried the hopes, in particular, of the smaller nations.

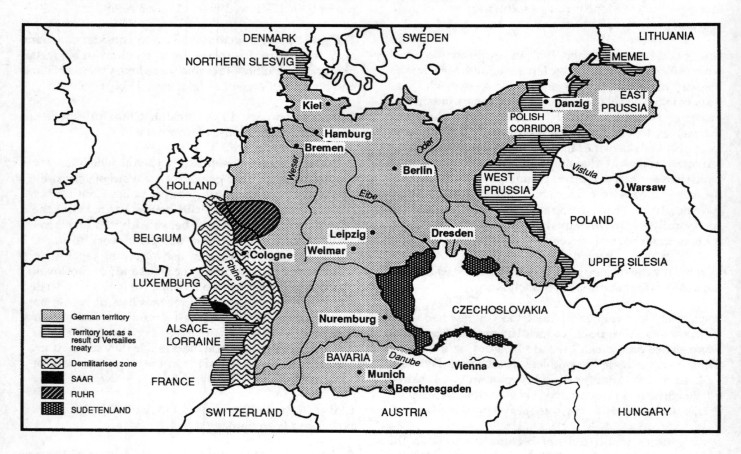

Wiemar Germany - 1919 -1933

When Adolf Hitler was invited to become Chancellor of Germany in January 1933 Japan's actions in the Far East had already shown the weakness of collective security as a means of resisting aggression. Hitler's writing and speeches made it clear that he would follow a very aggressive foreign policy, the aims of which had been laid down in Nazi Party documents as early as 1920.

AIMS OF HITLER'S FOREIGN POLICY

The Nazis demanded the union of all Germans to form a 'Great Germany'. In the 19th century, German nationalists had argued over whether they should aim for a 'Gross Deutchland' (or Greater Germany), including the Austrians and all the other Germans, or settle for a 'Klein Deutschland' (little Germany) excluding Austria.

On the first page of *Mein Kampf* Hitler wrote:

> "German-Austria must return to the great German mother country... One blood demands one Reich... Only when the Reich borders include the very last German, but can no longer guarantee his daily bread, will the moral right to acquire foreign soil arise from the distress of our people."
> (Adolf Hitler, *Mein Kampf* translated by R Mannheim , p.3)

Although the Treaty of Versailles had specifically forbidden the Anschluss, or Union of Austria and Germany, Hitler was determined to create a 'Gross Deutchland' which encompassed not only his Austrian homeland but also united the German minorities now subject to the rule of

Czechoslovakia, Poland and other states. The Nazi slogan "Ein Volk, Ein Reich, Ein Führer" (one people, one empire, one leader) had many implications.

In an open letter to Chancellor Bruning in 1931 Hitler wrote of the Treaty of Versailles:

> "I was of the conviction that without a complete abolition of reparations it was not possible to conceive any restoration to economic health."
> "The Treaty of Versailles is no Peace Treaty. On the contrary it belongs to the category of those Tribute-Diktats which bear in themselves the seed of later wars."
> "The demand for the abolition of those clauses of the Versailles Treaty which reduce our people both in the sphere of law and economics to folk of the second class is not only our moral will but our moral duty."
> (*The Speeches of Adolf Hitler* edited by Norman Baynes, p.998)

When Hitler came to power the detested reparations payments, whereby Germany had to compensate the victors of the Great War for the damage they had endured, had been waived. This must have infuriated him since he would have derived immense personal satisfaction from repudiating them. However, in their rise to power the Nazis had made much capital out of the discriminatory nature of the disarmament clauses of the treaty:
- Germany and not France was forced to disarm
- Germany lost territory in Europe, where self-determination seemed to have been applied to everybody but the Germans

- all German colonies had been confiscated on the grounds that Germans were morally unsuited to ruling "native peoples".

The Nazis also fanned resentment of the moralistic way in which Germany had been lectured, in the "War Guilt Clause", for her role in causing the war. In an article for the *Sunday Express* in September 1930 he wrote:

> "We, the National Socialists, demand the revision of the Treaty of Versailles."
> "We demand the return of the Polish Corridor..."
> "All this is founded on the hypocritical basis that Germany was guilty of causing the World War. The National Socialists reject that accusation."
> (*The Speeches of Adolf Hitler* edited by N Baynes p. 995)

Hitler demanded land and colonies in which Germany's surplus population could be settled. In *Mein Kampf* (written 1924-25) he called for "Lebensraum" or living space.

> "Only an adequately large space on earth assures a nation of freedom of existence." (p.587)
> "The National Socialist Movement ... must find the courage to gather our people and their strength for an advance along the road that will lead this people from its present restricted living space to new land and soil, and hence also free it from the danger of vanishing from the earth or of serving others as a slave nation..." (p.590)
> "Land and soil is the goal of our foreign policy..." (p.593)
> "State boundaries are made by man and changed by man" (p.596)
> "If we speak of soil in Europe today, we can primarily have in mind only Russia and her vassal border states." (p.598)
> (Adolph Hitler, *Mein Kampf* translated by R Mannheim)

This had its basis in Hitler's racial creed. In *Mein Kampf* he argued that the whole history of mankind was a struggle between the races. This struggle, by a crudely Darwinian 'survival of the fittest' process, had produced the Aryan (Germanic) race which combined "robust muscular power with first class intellect". Hitler claimed it was the duty of the "Herrenvolk" or master-race to take over eastern Europe as far as the Ural Mountains, dispossessing the "Untermenschen" (the "inferior" Slavs, Russians, Poles, Ukrainians etc.) and using them and the resources of the area for the exclusive benefit of the Aryans. Only in this way could humanity progress.

Mein Kampf also shows Hitler's hatred of France and his desire to inflict on her Germany's revenge for defeat in the Great War. To do this he hoped for alliances with Britain and Italy which would enable him to counteract and dismantle the French system of alliances in eastern Europe established in the twenties.

HITLER : OPPORTUNIST OR GRAND STRATEGIST?

At the end of the Second World War it was accepted that Hitler had sought war as an act of policy and was therefore personally responsible for what happened. The leaders of Britain and France were condemned for failing to stand up to him and for not stopping him before he grew too strong. These ideas were thankfully accepted in Germany where few wanted to share with their Führer the blame for starting the war.

Since 1961 a controversy has raged in academic circles as to whether Hitler came to power with a fixed progamme in mind for achieving his foreign policy aims or whether he merely pursued age old German ambitions and took his chances when they arose, presented to him by inept statesmanship on the part of the leaders of Britain, France and the USA. The arguments on both sides are nicely summarised in *The Third Reich* by DG Williams (pub. Longmans 1982, pages 41-42). The controversy was started when the English Historian, AJP Taylor, claimed, in *Origins of the Second World War*, that Hitler merely wanted to make Germany Europe's leading power and that he seized each opportunity that was presented to him to strengthen her position. He did this by following foreign policy aims which the German Foreign Ministry had pursued since the time of Bismarck in the 1870s. Taylor doubts the existence of a master plan to take over and dominate Europe and the world by stages, culminating in the Second World War. Taylor implied that Hitler was not uniquely wicked and that his foreign policy was consistently German. Professor Fritz Fischer, perhaps the most influential figure in post war German historical thinking, has also argued that much of Hitler's foreign policy was part of a continuum dating back to the days of the Kaiserreich.

In response to this, the German 'programme school' of historians claims that Hitler came to power with the intention of following through a clearly defined programme of expansion and conquest. In the first phase Britain and Italy would act as allies while Germany defeated France and Russia, thus building up a huge continental power base. In the second phase it might have been necessary to dispense with Britain as the navy was enlarged, colonies were acquired and the USA was subjugated. Professors Andreas Hillgruber and Klaus Hildebrand are prominent in this school of thought.

Professor Alan Bullock has put forward a compromise theory that Hitler did have a series of foreign policy objectives and that he waited for the other great powers to present him with opportunities to achieve these one by one rather than attempting to adhere to a precise programme.

Sir Neville Henderson, Britain's ambassador to Berlin just before the outbreak of war had this to say:

> "Hitler is an Austrian, and the best known trait of the Austrians is their 'Schlamperei'- a sort of happy-go-lucky and haphazard way of doing things. I always felt that Hitler had his full share of this characteristic. He had all sorts of general plans in his head, but I greatly doubt if he had preconceived ideas as to how they were to be executed. Unfortunately, as he went on he became more and more intoxicated with success and confident in his own greatness and infallibility. His plans grew more grandiose, and he combined his 'Schlamperei' with an amazing mastery of opportunism... Hitler waited until his opponents made a tactical mistake, and then used the plan which seemed best to suit both

his own general objective and the opportunity afforded by the mistake."

(from *Failure of a Mission* (published 1940), p. 185. Quoted in *National Socialism in Germany* by Niall Rothnie)

This controversy is not unique in German history. A similar debate exists over the process whereby Otto von Bismarck, Chancellor of Prussia, united Germany in 1871. Benjamin Disraeli, the British Prime Minister, claimed that before the events occurred Bismarck outlined to him how his wars against Denmark (1864), Austria (1866) and France (1870) would facilitate the unification of Germany under Prussia. In these wars Bismarck employed a diplomatic strategy of isolating each successive enemy from all potential allies before unleashing the Prussian army in a deadly lightning war. Almost seventy years later Hitler was to use a similar strategy in dealing with Austria and Czechoslovakia.

THE FAILURE OF THE LEAGUE'S DISARMAMENT CONFERENCE

When in power Hitler always took great care to avoid appearing as a simple aggressive megalomaniac. In each crisis he showed great skill in presenting Germany as the aggrieved party and in creating the impression that he was a peaceful man acting in defence of the German people. Thus, in his early speeches as Chancellor, he expressed a willingness to disarm and to co-operate with other nations if only they would disarm to the levels that Germany had already achieved. In February 1932 the League of Nations had finally got a disarmament conference under way in Geneva. In May 1933 Hitler demanded parity in armaments with the French. He knew that they would never agree to this regardless of the level of armaments proposed, since they were acutely aware of their inferior industrial resources and smaller population and were obsessed with security as a direct result of invasions by Germany in 1870 and 1914. This enabled Hitler to withdraw Germany from both the Conference and the League in October 1933 claiming that these organisations were merely a French conspiracy to keep Germany a second-rate power, incapable of self-defence. Many British politicians were openly sympathetic and were convinced by these arguments because they felt guilty about the severity of the Treaty of Versailles. Thus Hitler's gamble that the embarrassment of his enemies at the apparent justice of his cause would prevent the League from acting against him paid off. This was the first of many successful gambles. He continued to make peaceful noises, offering to disarm or to conclude non-aggression pacts but of course he got no response. In November a plebiscite showed that the German people overwhelmingly supported his moves.

In March 1934 the published German military budget showed substantial increases, indicating that Germany was rearming. The following month the League's Disarmament Conference was disbanded.

The diplomatic world was astounded in January 1934 by the announcement of a non-aggression pact between Germany and Poland. No other part of the Versailles Treaty was resented more in Germany than the Polish territorial settlement which had placed a million Germans under Polish government and separated East Prussia from the rest of Germany. Even Gustav Stresemann had been unwilling to guarantee this frontier although he had accepted Germany's western frontier by the Treaty of Locarno in 1925. Now Hitler was making dove like noises. Poles and Germans would have to learn to live together.

May 23, 1934

THE CONFERENCE EXCUSES ITSELF.

Peace was guaranteed for ten years. In reality there wasn't much Hitler could do about Poland at that stage so he made a virtue out of necessity and signed the 1934 pact which helped to detach Poland from its 1921 pact with France. Yet another crack had appeared in the collective security system.

Up to mid-1934 Hitler had hardly put a foot wrong in his conduct of foreign affairs, although German rearmament was a cause for concern in many nations. Anschluss, the Union of Hitler's homeland of Austria with Germany, had always been an important plank in the Nazi platform. Since coming to power the Nazis had financed and encouraged the Austrian Nazi party led by Alfred Eduard Frauenfeld. Similar support was given to Nazi parties among German minorities in other parts of Europe such as the Sudetenland of Czechoslovakia. The Austrian Nazis ran a campaign of intimidation, terrorism and violent propaganda of such intensity that the neo-fascist Chancellor of Austria, Englebert Dollfuss, had the party suppressed. On 25th July 1934 the Nazis assassinated Dollfuss as part of an attempted coup d'état intended to force the union with Germany . International alarm was widespread. Mussolini, who had no desire for a common frontier with Hitler, massed 100,000 troops on Italy's border with Austria. Hitler was taken aback by the intensity of the reaction he had caused and was forced to disown the Putsch. Although the Italian Fascists and the Nazis had similar ideologies, Mussolini was acutely aware that the South Tyrol, gained by Italy from Austria by the Treaty of St. Germain in 1919, had a substantial German minority. He also feared that Hitler would use Austria as a base to undermine Italy's influence in the Balkans.

German Rearmament, the Stresa Front & Soviet Reaction

In March 1935 Hermann Göring, a flying ace of the Great War and one of Hitler's ministers, revealed the existence of the Luftwaffe (airforce) and general conscription to the armed forces was reintroduced. Both these actions were in direct contradiction of the Versailles Treaty and in the wake of the Austrian debacle they produced a hurried attempt to reassert collective security. In April the French promoted a conference at Stresa in Italy attended by the Prime Ministers and Foreign Ministers of France, Britain and Italy. A formal protest against Hitler's flouting of the disarmament clauses of the Treaty of Versailles was issued. The 'Stresa Front' was, however, to be a short-lived phenomenon, wrecked by the quarrel which arose from Italy's invasion of Abyssinia.

The Soviet Union also thought that Hitler's behaviour was threatening. In September 1934 she joined the League of Nations and the following May she signed a Mutual Assistance Pact with France. Thus in a remarkably short time, Hitler had both isolated Germany and united the great powers against him . Sadly this unity was not to last.

Arms Appeasement: The Anglo-German Naval Agreement

Even while the Stresa discussions were taking place, Britain was busy undermining them. In response to rumours about the Luftwaffe in February 1935, Britain had suggested to Germany that she might like to join an Anglo-French air pact. The British attitude to German rearmament was to try and limit it by negotiation rather than stop it by force or threat. The negotiations thus begun eventually produced a bomb-shell in the form of the Anglo-German Naval agreement of 1935. Without consulting her friends (both France and Italy were naval powers in their own right) Britain agreed that Germany could build up to 35% of her naval strength and she could equal the submarine strength of the British Empire despite the fact that the Treaty of Versailles had forbidden Germany to have any U-boats at all. The effect of this agreement was shattering. The French and Italians felt that Britain was unpredictable and unreliable and likely to make conflicting agreements with her friends and her notional enemies. This was a poor basis for a strong stance against Nazi aggression.

3 THE ABYSSINIAN AFFAIR

The Stresa Front provided Britain and France with only a brief period of peace of mind. The dispute which would destroy it had already begun to develop when the Front was formed. Italy's invasion of Abyssinia in October 1935 was to shatter the common resolve against Hitler.

Half a century later it is hard to understand why any country would want Abyssinia, now called Ethiopia, as a colony. In the mid-1980s its public image was of a ruined, drought-stricken, strife-torn patch of semidesert dependent on Band-Aid and international relief agencies for its day-to-day survival. Today no developed country would accept it as a colony, but it wasn't always like that. In 1934 it had a much smaller population, much more forest cover and was much less susceptible to drought. The 'scramble for Africa' in the second half of the nineteenth century had left only two territories independent of European rule, Liberia in the west and Abyssinia in the east. Abyssinia was a natural target for any country in search of an empire. It was different from the rest of Africa in many ways, being a mountain empire ruled by a Christian, Semitic, Amharic-speaking dynasty which claimed descent from the Queen of Sheba , an Abyssinian, and King Solomon of Israel to whom she had paid an early state visit. The Emperors honoured themselves with the title of 'King of Kings,Lion of the tribes of Judah'. The Ethiopian Christian church dates from the 4th century AD and has close connections with the Egyptian coptic church. Its most impressive relics are the magnificent churches carved out of solid rock at Aksum. Moslem Somalis and spirit worshipping Hamitic tribes were also among the Emperor's subjects.

Britain had encouraged Italy to take an interest in the area in the late nineteenth century. It occupied a vital position on the sea route to India and the British had no desire to see it controlled by a first-rate power like the French or the Germans. As a new state which had only emerged into unity in 1870, Italy, like Germany, had entered the scramble for Africa late and had had to content herself with the last few scraps of territory. In the 1880s she occupied Abyssinia's northern coastal province of Eritrea but when Italian troops moved inland they ran into serious difficulties. At Adowa in 1896 the Italians achieved the distinction of becoming the first European nation to suffer a defeat, which they were unable to avenge, at the hands of an African nation . The 100,000 strong army of the Emperor Menelik II overwhelmed 25,000 Italians, killing 6,000 and holding the rest to ransom. Italy joined Britain and France in 1906 in an agreement to maintain Abyssinia's independence, a treaty which was reinforced by the 1928 Italo-Abyssinian Friendship and Non-Aggression Treaty . In 1923 Italy's support secured membership of the League of Nations for Abyssinia despite British objections on the grounds that slavery and slave trading were still endemic there.

In 1930 Ras Tafari was crowned King of Kings, Lion of the tribe of Judah, the Emperor Haile Selassie I at Addis Ababa. Black people in America and the West Indies began to look to independent Abyssinia as a symbol of hope for the liberation of blacks from white rule and proof that black people could rule themselves. In the Caribbean there emerged the Rastafarian cult which survives to this day with the associated 'dreadlocks' of plaited hair and marijuana smoking. Haile Selassie, wishing to show that he was not going to be an Italian puppet, made a trade treaty with Japan and induced a sharp change in the direction of Italian policy in the region.

Mussolini had a number of reasons for seeking control of Abyssinia. Revenge for Adowa meant much to a man sworn to restore the glories of the Roman Empire and Italian self-respect. Italy lacked a large colonial empire, the outward sign of a great power. Mussolini's feelings about the way the Treaty of Versailles had redistributed Germany's colonies is evident from a speech he made in October 1935, reported in *Popolo d'Italia*.

> "When in 1915 Italy exposed itself to the risks of war and joined its destiny with that of the allies, how much praise there was for our courage and how many promises were made! But after the common victory to which Italy had made the supreme contribution of 670,000 dead, 400,000 mutilated, and a million wounded, around the hateful peace table Italy received but a few crumbs from the rich colonial booty gathered by others. We have been patient for thirteen years, during which the circle of selfishness which strangles our vitality has become tighter. With Abyssinia we have been patient for forty years! It is time to say enough!"

(from *A History of Modern Italy* by Clough and Saladino p.491)

The Duce looks down on Adowa : A 16-ft head carved from the rock

The Italian economy was not in perfect shape. A colonial

war would distract public attention from this fact and Abyssinia could become a useful market for Italian goods and a place to settle Italy's surplus population which tended to be lost to Italy through emigration to the USA. Above all Mussolini glorified warfare: *"A day on the battlefield is worth a thousand years of peace"*; *"Better to live for a day as a lion than a lifetime as a sheep"*; *"War is to men what child bearing is to women."* These Fascist slogans illustrate his belief that war would produce a tougher, more disciplined Italy. The experience of battle would improve the whole nation.

The frontier between British Somaliland and Abyssinia had never been clearly defined. A similar situation existed between Abyssinia and Italian Somaliland. In December 1934 a Boundary Commission, consisting of British and Abyssinian surveyors, together with a bodyguard of six hundred local troops, arrived at the water hole at Wal Wal, well inside what was agreed to be Abyssinian territory. There they found a body of 200 Italian Somali troops encamped near some wells which they had been allowed to use since 1928. The Italian native troops began to insult the Abyssinians who resented their presence on Abyssinian territory. The British left in a hurry. Two days later the Abyssinians tried to rush the Italians but were driven back by machine guns, armoured cars and aircraft. Their commander was among the dead, as were thirty two of the Italians' Somali soldiers.

Haile Selassie proposed arbitration in the dispute but Mussolini demanded compensation and also that Abyssinian troops should salute the Italian flag at Wal Wal knowing full well that such a proud people would never agree to this. Since his country had joined the League in 1924 Haile Selassie turned to this body for independent arbitration.

The Manchurian episode had shown that the League did not act with undue haste. In July 1935 its investigators cleverly fudged the issue by reporting that neither side was to blame for the Wal Wal incident since both believed they had a right to use the oasis. Unfortunately Mussolini was not willing to let the matter rest there. He had been making preparations for invasion.

After the Wal Wal incident the Italian ambassador in London, Dino Grandi, was told to sound out the British government on two matters. Were they willing to let Mussolini have Abyssinia? Were they willing to help him defend Austria's independence against Hitler? At a lunch party Ramsay McDonald, the Prime Minister, is alleged to have said "England is a lady. A lady's taste is for vigorous action in the male, but she likes things done discreetly, not in public. Be tactful and we will have no objections." Mussolini took this to be the green light on Abyssinia. McDonald was less helpful about Austria which he regarded as "a ripe fruit ready to fall to Germany". Britain, in fact, had little sympathy for Abyssinia, having opposed her entry to the League on the grounds that slavery was rife there.

Pierre Laval, the French Foreign Minister, visited Rome in January 1935. The French were anxious to unite Europe against the Hitler threat so to please the Italians he gave them part of French Somaliland, bordering Abyssinia, and sold them France's shares in the Abyssinian Railway which ran from Djibouti in French Somaliland to Addis Ababa.

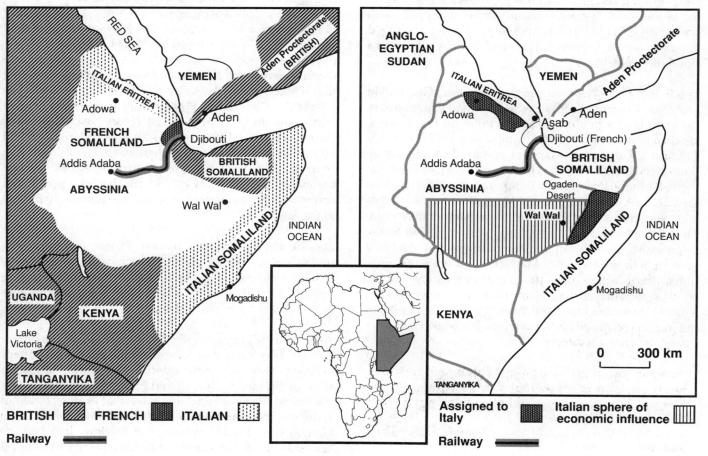

Abyssinia (1935) and her neighbours

BRITISH   FRENCH   ITALIAN

Railway

The Hoare-Laval pact

Assigned to Italy

Italian sphere of economic influence

Railway

Although Laval later claimed that he was giving support for economic and not military plans Mussolini again felt that he had the blessing of the western democracies for his venture and began to move large numbers of Italian troops and military supplies through the Anglo-French controlled Suez Canal to his bases at Massawa and Mogadishu.

Ramsay McDonald retired, due to ill health, and was replaced by Stanley Baldwin as Prime Minister of the National Government in June 1935. The 'Peace Ballot' organised by the League had shown that ten million voters in Britain thought that sanctions should be used against aggressors. Anthony Eden, the new Minister for League of Nations Affairs, had no desire to encourage flagrant violation of the League's principles so he went to Italy and suggested that he could arrange for part of the Ogaden desert, with its Somali population, to be transferred from Abyssinia to Italian Somaliland. This area could also have the use of the port of Zeila, in British Somaliland, which was connected to its hinterland by a 'camel track'. Mussolini, who already had 100,000 square miles of the Sahara in Libya was unco-operative saying, "I am not a collector of deserts!" [See Source 2]

On September 4th 1935 the Italians told the League that "Abyssinia is a barbarous and uncivilised state, who by her conduct has placed herself outside the League". A month later they claimed that her "warlike and aggressive spirit " had "imposed war on Italy". The fighting began on 3rd October when Italy invaded Abyssinia without declaring war.

In order to overcome the Italians' wholesome distaste for war a vigorous fascist campaign had promised a "war without tears" secured by "modern methods", such as tanks, aircraft and gas, as well as glory and riches. Facing the enthusiastic Italians was an 'army' equipped with spears and 1874 model French étienne rifles which betrayed the marksman's position with a vivid flash by night and a cloud of smoke by day .

The Italian plan was for a 'pincer campaign'. One Italian army was to march south from Massawa in Eritrea under the commander in chief General Emilio de Bono while another pushed north from Mogadishu under General Grazziani. Progress was slow at first until the elderly de Bono (aged 66) was replaced by the young at heart General Pietro Badoglio (65) who got things moving. Nevertheless, the war took an embarrassingly long time as the Italians had to build roads for their transport wherever they went. Thus the international community was subjected to the unpleasant spectacle of the long drawn out death of Abyssinia. It was not until May 1936 that it was all over. Italian 'civilisation', mustard gas, machine guns and the bombing of villages, had triumphed over savage Africa. Vittorio Mussolini, one of the dictator's sons, was a pilot in the war and recorded his impressions in a book, *Flying over Ethiopian Mountain Ranges*.

> "magnificent sport ... one group of horsemen gave me the impression of a budding rose unfolding as the bombs fell in their midst and blew them up. It was exceptionally good fun."
> (Quoted by C Leeds, *Italy under Mussolini*, quoting Laura Fermi, *Mussolini*)

Convinced that Adowa had proved them invincible the Abyssinians consistently took the wrong course of action. They tried to take on the Italians in pitched battles instead of fighting a guerrilla war until the April rains played havoc with mechanised transport. By prolonging the war they might have embarrassed the international community into action but this seems doubtful. Britain and France were far too concerned not to make an enemy of Mussolini or drive him into an alliance with Hitler.

This horrid little war had enormous international implications. It completed the wrecking of the League and finally threw Hitler and Mussolini together thus making the Second World War possible.

On 6th October the Italians captured Adowa and avenged their old defeat. The next day the League condemned their aggression and announced economic sanctions. The war was in its fifth day. By its own standards the League had acted with great alacrity.

Under article 16 of the Charter, member states were asked to forbid all loans to Italy, cease all trade with her in arms or war materials and ban all Italian imports. Member states were not supposed to sell war materials to the Abyssinians either, since they were also considered to be a belligerent nation. Germany, having left the League in 1933, sold her 16,000 rifles and 600 machine guns. This was Hitler's revenge for Italian opposition to the Anschluss. America's President Roosevelt invoked his country's neutrality laws and ordered an embargo on arms sales to both sides.

In 1935 Russia continued to trade with Italy while Austria, Switzerland, Albania and Hungary also refused to implement sanctions. Nor was any attempt made to deny Italy supplies of oil or coal although she had neither of these vital resources. Mussolini later admitted that oil sanctions would have forced him out of Abyssinia in a few days. The French, in particular, were very reluctant to employ this measure since they did not want to do anything that would offend Mussolini and drive him into alliance with Hitler. Pierre Laval, Foreign Minister of France, argued that it should be kept as a last resort. "Italy", he said, "would regard oil sanctions as an act of war and might attack the British fleet in the Mediterranean or Egypt as a reprisal." Iron, steel and copper were not regarded as war materials and were never on the list of prohibited commodities. No attempt was made to deny Italy the use of the Suez canal.

Despite the half-hearted nature of these sanctions, the Italian press howled about their harshness. Ordinary Italians were persuaded to surrender their gold wedding rings to help finance the war. Steel replacements were issued as a mark of patriotism.

As early as September 1935, Sir Samuel Hoare, the British Foreign Secretary, had agreed with Laval that military sanctions were out of the question. Although Abyssinia was surrounded by British and French colonies and they controlled the Suez canal it was felt that France could not spare the men from the defence of her vital border with Germany. Britain, whose war machine had become seriously run down, could not afford to weaken her naval strength in the North Sea, where it watched the Germans, by diverting ships to the Mediterranean to hold Suez against the Italians. The Royal Navy also had to bear in mind the possibility of war against Japan. Admiral Sir Ernle Chatfield, First Sea Lord and Chairman of the Chiefs of Staffs Committee, informed his political masters in the British Government that none of the services was in a fit state to fight the Italians at that juncture. [See Source 3] Britain was the world's greatest Imperial power in 1935 and was well accustomed to suppressing and subjugating Africans and Asians. Few British, or French, ministers saw anything morally wrong with what the Italians were doing.

In December Hoare went to Paris and met Laval. Both men wanted to end the conflict and at the same time keep Mussolini's friendship. They agreed to offer him the province of Tigre, to be added to the Italian colony of Eritrea in the North. In the South the Ogaden desert was to be added to Italian Somaliland. Furthermore, the Italians were to have economic rights over a large area in the southern part of the Empire, effectively making southern Abyssinia an Italian Protectorate. The rest of the country, the most fertile part, would be independent. The Italians were expected to hand over the Eritrean port of Assab to the Abyssinians to provide them with an outlet to the sea. Assab wasn't much of a port and the road joining it to its proposed hinterland was contemptuously described by *The Times*, rarely a critic of appeasement, as "a corridor for camels". Moreover, the Italians wanted to keep it. Naturally the Abyssinians had not been consulted about these proposals.

(Appeasement is the idea that peace can sometimes be preserved by making concessions to an aggrieved or aggressor state. The essence of the Hoare-Laval pact was that Italy should be bought off by offering her part of Abyssinia, an idea wholly alien to the philosophy of the League.)

Before the plan could be put into effect, the press got wind of the details causing a storm of indignation in both countries and forcing Hoare to resign on 18th December. Laval's administration lasted another fortnight. Duff Cooper, Secretary of State for War and critic of appeasement, later wrote in his book *Old Men Forget*:

"Rumours were rife of the terrible strength of the Italian navy and of the 'mad-dog act' to which further irritation might drive the Duce ..."
"But before the Duce had time to declare himself (ie. on the plan) there arose a howl of indignation from the people of Britain... During my experience of politics I never witnessed so devastating a wave of public indignation. That outburst swept Sir Samuel Hoare from office."(pp 191-3)

Defending himself in the Commons shortly before his resignation, Hoare said,

"... the threat of war and the outbreak of war has raised very difficult questions between ourselves and France. It must have been obvious to every Hon. Member that a great body of opinion in France was intensely nervous of a breech with Italy, was intensely nervous of anything likely to weaken French defence... I did everything in my power to make a settlement possible ... while loyally continuing a policy of sanctions and coercive action ..." (*Hansard*)

Duff Cooper had a certain sympathy for Hoare even if he did not go as far as supporting him.

"...the British, who fight with the most glorious courage and the toughest tenacity, have such a horror of war that they will never support a policy which entails the slightest risk of it. ... The British people were very angry with Mussolini and very sorry for the Emperor of Abyssinia, but they were not willing to give grounds for war to the former or effective help to the latter. Sir Samuel Hoare and Monsieur Pierre Laval sought to give shape to these sentiments by an agreement which, while handing over the substance of Abyssinia to Italy, would have left a shadowy remnant to the Emperor."
(from *Old Men Forget* by Duff Cooper, p. 192)

In its 1935 election manifesto Britain's National Government had maintained that the League of Nations was "the cornerstone of British foreign policy". It now seemed to many that the British were willing to contemplate all sorts of shady deals with aggressors rather than promoting, and co-operating in, an international policy to control aggression. In addition, Hoare had clearly underestimated the will of the British people to resist aggression and the importance they attached to the League. The results of its Peace Ballot, an opinion poll which the League had held, had been published in June 1935. They showed that 58% of those interviewed thought that military sanctions should be used against an unrepentant aggressor. Over 90% of respondents thought that economic sanctions should be used to prevent wars. Does the result of the Peace Ballot contradict Duff Cooper's remarks on British public opinion? In Duff Cooper's view

"...we had little to fear. Italy had no allies. Germany would not and could not then have raised a finger to assist her. All the smaller powers that were members of the League were pledged to aid us, and between them they controlled the whole of the Mediterranean seaboard that was not actually in Italian hands. Can we believe that the mad dog would have been mad enough to go to war against such odds? Can we doubt that had he done so he would have been muzzled for life? It would have been the end of Mussolini and the end of Fascism, a triumph for the League and a warning to the Nazis.
If there had been a great leader in a high position at that time he might have rallied the country to the support of such a policy, and if Great Britain had led, the smaller nations would have followed."
(from *Old Men Forget* p.192)

Since Britain and France were the League's two most powerful supporters, this scandal undermined the sanctions campaign and other nations ceased to implement it. The smaller nations, in particular, lost faith in the League and felt the need to look to larger powers for protection. A British naval squadron was sent to Alexandria in Egypt, but it was too late. The damage had already been done. From this point onwards, the great powers abandoned the pretence of solving disputes through the

League and resorted to old-fashioned diplomacy and power block politics. The policy favoured by the Western Democracies was increasingly one of appeasement. The League was now clearly a 'dead duck'. Hitler must have noted how, as in the Manchurian Crisis, Britain and France had appeared weak, indecisive and unwilling to act. This apparent weakness may have encouraged him to act aggressively in later crises.

Haile Selassie appeared before the Assembly of the League and, to the derisive whistles of Italian journalists, made a dignified appeal for help for his embattled nation. None was forthcoming despite the intense embarrassment his speech caused. Later he said, "Today it is us, tomorrow it will be you !"

Mussolini's Abyssinian adventure caused Germany and Italy to draw closer together. In October 1936 they agreed to preserve the independence of Austria. Promises like this came easily to Hitler and he would honour them for as long as it was convenient. Mussolini called the agreement "the Rome-Berlin Axis around which can revolve all those European powers with a will to collaboration and peace".

November 1937 saw Italy joining Japan and Germany in the anti-comintern pact, an alliance which was ostensibly against the spread of international communism.

The following month Mussolini pulled Italy out of the League and, although Britain and France both recognised her regime in Abyssinia in 1938, the Stresa Front was one of the more obvious casualties in this last chapter of the scramble for Africa.

The latest addition to the empire of Victor Emmanuel III was to prove a real disappointment to Italy. Mussolini felt that too few Italians, only 1,537, had died in the struggle to achieve the hardening of the national character he so desired. By 1939 Abyssinia still took only 2% of Italy's trade and and there were ten times as many Italians in New York as there were in all of Italy's colonies. Finally, during the Second World War the Italians were evicted by British, Indian, Kenyan, Nigerian, South African and other troops. A book entitled *Springbok Victory* describes how the South African army went through the Italians "like the Springbok pack through a club eight".

4 HITLER'S FOREIGN POLICY: THE RHINELAND

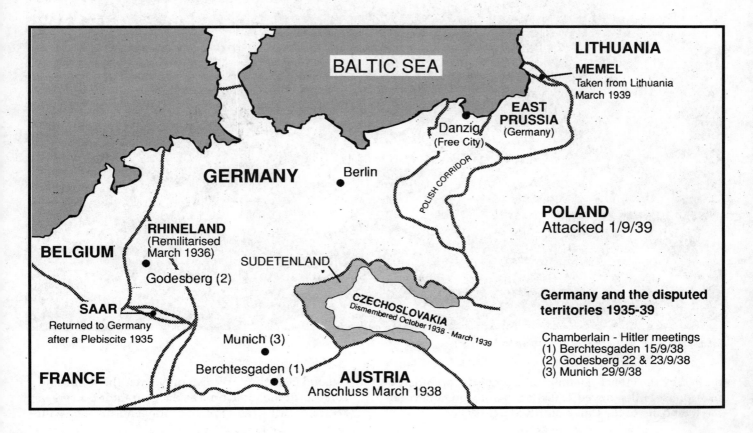

In January 1935 the League held a plebiscite in the Saar to determine the future of the Saar coalfield, whose production had gone to France since 1919. Ninety percent voted for the return of the territory to Germany.

Early in 1936 Hitler turned his attention to another part of his western frontier, the Rhineland. Under the Treaty of Versailles this area had been demilitarised. No military installations or garrisons were permitted on the left bank or within 50 kilometres of the right (east) bank of the River Rhine. This was to give France a sense of security. The moment German troops entered this area France could regard it as a sign of imminent invasion and take action to ensure that any fighting occurred on German soil. The French were barely satisfied with this. They would have preferred an independent Rhenish Republic. The Rhineland situation left Germany in a position of weakness against France. The Abyssinian affair, which shattered the unity of the Stresa Front, gave Hitler the chance to do something about it. He rightly assumed that Britain, and perhaps even France, was too busy worrying about Mussolini to pay much attention to him. [See Source 8] As a result of the Hoare-Laval fiasco, relations between the two governments were badly strained to the point where concerted action from them was most improbable. Due to tensions with Italy, the French had been moving large numbers of troops away from their frontier with Germany. One-fifth of the army had been sent to the Alps and Tunisia.

In May 1935 Hitler protested that the Franco-Soviet Mutual Assistance Treaty violated the spirit of the Locarno Pact and threatened Germany with encirclement. Speaking to the Reichstag on 7th March 1936 he said:

"To this (the Locarno) Pact Germany made a contribution which represented a great sacrifice; because while France fortified her frontier with steel and concrete and armaments, and garrisoned it heavily, a condition of complete defencelessness was imposed upon us on our Western frontier."

"France has not concluded this Treaty with a European power of no significance. ... Soviet Russia is the exponent of a revolutionary political and philosophical system ... Its political creed is ... world revolution. It cannot be foreseen whether this philosophy will not be victorious ... in France as well. But should this happen ... then ... this new Bolshevik state would be a section of the Bolshevik International, which means that decisions as to aggression or non-aggression would not be taken in two different states ... , but orders would be issued from one headquarters, ... not in Paris but in Moscow."

"This gigantic mobilisation of the East against Central Europe is opposed not only to the letter but above all to the spirit of the Locarno Pact."
(Norman Baynes (ed), *The Speeches of Adolf Hitler* p. 1287-'91)

The treaty was not universally popular in France either, where the right disliked any association with a communist power. It was not until 27th February 1936 that it was

German troops marching across the Hohenzollen bridge

ratified by the French Chamber of Deputies (Parliament). In response Hitler moved 22,000 troops into towns beyond the west bank of the Rhine on 7th March 1936.

Hitler had been warned by his army that they were not strong enough to push ahead with remilitarisation should the French resist. Hitler accepted this and said later that "the 48 hours after the march into the Rhineland were the most nerve-wracking of my life. If the French had then marched into the Rhineland, we would have had to withdraw with our tails between our legs." Hitler's move had taken neither the British nor the French by surprise. They had been expecting this for some time, especially since Nazi paramilitary units had already entered the demilitarised zone. When remilitarisation came, however, the allies showed a complete lack of preparation. French confidence had been badly shaken by their disastrous invasion of the Ruhr in 1923, when they had acted without British support. Moreover, by 1936 political opinion had become drastically polarised between left and right and national unity had suffered as a result. In February 1934 there had been serious rioting in Paris which looked suspiciously like an attempted coup d'état by the neo-fascist groups Action français, Jeunesses Patriotes and Solidarité Française. The government was anxious to avoid any repetition of this event.

The French right felt that Hitler had been needlessly provoked by the treaty with Russia. Leading French generals advised their government that the army could not take action on its own. They reported that the Germans were on the point of overtaking them in terms of military equipment and appear to have grossly overestimated the number of German troops in the area. Chiefs of staff of the French armed services met on the day after the remilitarisation.

General Gamelin: "We can only enter the Rhineland zone ... at the same time as the guarantor powers of Locarno British and Italian contingents must be with us and the Belgians ...
Admiral Durand-Viel : At the moment England could give us nothing but moral support. Before anything more the Ethiopian affair would have to be liquidated. It is impossible to envisage common action with two powers (Britain and Italy) which are themselves in a state of reciprocal hostility. When this hostility is ended, at least a fortnight will be needed before British naval forces are ready to act in the North sea and the Channel. At present the British Isles are deprived of any naval protection."
(From *Documents Diplomatiques Francais, 1932-1939*, 2nd series, 1936-9, vol 1. no 334. Quoted by Anthony Adamthwaite in *The Making of the Second World War*. p. 155)

Between 1929 and 1934 impressive defensive fortifications, known as the Maginot line, had been constructed along France's border with Germany. The line was designed to give security against invasion, but it turned the French army into a 'static force' with a defensive mentality and no desire to move forward from its concrete bunkers and case hardened steel gun cupolas (domes).

France looked to Britain for support but found only the will to denounce what Hitler had done. Many influential men in British politics shared the views of the French right that the Franco-Soviet treaty had unduly provoked Hitler. There was concern about Nazi aggression but it was hoped that a conciliatory approach might persuade Germany to re-enter the League and resume disarmament talks. *[See Source 4]* Some British ministers felt that the military defeat of Hitler could lead to a communist takeover in Germany. There was a persistent belief that Germany had been too severely chastised at Versailles and that something had to be done to redress the balance. The influential Lord Lothian said "...they are only going into their own back garden" and Stanley Baldwin felt that military intervention would be "out of proportion to what Germany had done".

Writing in 1962 Anthony Eden said:

"Hitler's occupation of the Rhineland was an occasion when the British and French governments should have attempted the impossible. Academically speaking, there is little doubt that Hitler should have been called to order, if need be forcibly, at his first breach of an international agreement. But nobody was prepared to do it, in this country literally nobody; even the most warlike proclaimed that the League Council must be called, which would not have endorsed the use of force..."

(*Facing the Dictators.* Quoted by Martin Gilbert in *Britain and Germany between the Wars*)

March 7th 1936 fell on a Saturday and almost everybody of importance in Britain and France had gone off to enjoy a weekend break. Hitler believed that when they arrived back at their desks on the Monday his reoccupation of the Rhineland would be a fait accompli and they would feel that it was too late to act. He was right.

As troops marched into the Rhineland German ambassadors issued a memorandum to all interested governments. It justified remilitarisation and, characteristically, made a number of offers:

"(1) The German Government declare themselves prepared to enter at once into negotiations with France and Belgium on the creation of a zone demilitarised on both sides, and to give their agreement in advance on such a proposal, whatever its depth and effect, on condition of full parity.

... (7) Now that Germany's equality of rights and the restoration of full sovereignty over the entire territory of the German Reich has been finally attained, the German Government considers the chief reason for their withdrawal from the League of Nations to have been removed. They are therefore prepared to return to the League of Nations. ... the separation of the Covenant of the League of Nations from its Versailles setting will be clarified through friendly negotiations ..."

(*Documents on German Foreign Policy* Ser. C, Vol. V Doc. 3)

These proposals seem reasonable enough at first sight but consider what the first one implies for the French and the £40 million spent on their defences. Hitler must have known it would never be considered. Talks dragged on but got nowhere, exactly as the Germans had intended.

Against the advice of his Generals, Hitler had successfully read the situation in Europe. *[See Source 9]* His standing in Germany was immeasurably enhanced by the reoccupation of the Rhineland as demonstrated by the near unanimous vote of approval by the German people of his policy on 29th March (see Table 4.1). Moreover, the French could no longer control him by the threat of invasion. Another gamble had paid off and Hitler's Germany was much stronger as a result. With his western frontier secured, he could turn his attention to the east.

Total of Qualified Voters	45,453,691
Total of Votes Cast	45,001,489 (99%)
Votes Cast Against or Invalid	540,211
Votes Cast for the List	44,461,278 (98.8%)

Table 4.1

"... Adolf Hitler was permitted to win the first battle of the Second World War without firing a shot. He, and only he, appreciated the issues at stake: that within eighteen months Germany would have over-topped Britain and France in armaments and that this was therefore the last occasion on which they could speak from strength; that the crumbling of the structure of Locarno would result in the falling away of Belgium to neutrality and the consequent jeopardising of the Allied left flank in the event of war; that all the treaty commitments linking France with her European allies, Poland and Czechoslovakia, had become, at one blow, far more difficult to carry out, since France would now have to batter her way into Germany through a system of fortifications set up against the Maginot Line. The year 1936 marks the beginning of British rearmament and its chief protagonists were Mr Neville Chamberlain, Mr Anthony Eden and Mr Duff Cooper. Convinced that realities must be faced and that disarmament must follow and not precede the establishment of a sense of security,..."

(*Munich, Prologue to Tragedy* by J Wheeler Bennet, published by Macmillan)

However, not everyone sees it in such straightforward terms.

"The seventh of March 1936 marked a turning point of history, but more in appearance than reality. In theory Germany's reoccupation of the Rhineland made it difficult, or even impossible, for France to aid her eastern allies, Poland and Czechoslovakia; in fact she had abandoned any such idea years ago ... The reoccupation of the Rhineland did not affect France from the defensive point of view. If the Maginot line were all it claimed to be, then her security was as great as before; if the Maginot line was no good, then France had never been secure in any case. Nor was the situation all loss for France. Germany, by reoccupying the Rhineland, used up the priceless asset which had brought her so many advantages; the asset of being disarmed ...

It was said at the time, and has often been said since, that 7 March 1936 was 'the last chance' ... when Germany could have been stopped without all the sacrifice and suffering of a great war. Technically, on paper, this was true: the French had a great army, and the Germans had none. Psychologically it was the reverse of the truth ... The French army could march into Germany; it could extract promises of good behaviour from the Germans, and then it would go away. The situation would remain the same as before, or, if anything worse – the Germans more resentful and restless than ever. There was in fact no sense in opposing Germany until there was something solid to oppose, until the settlement of Versailles was undone and Germany rearmed. Only a country which aims at victory can be threatened with defeat. 7 March was thus a double turning point. It opened the door for Germany's success. It also opened the door for her ultimate failure."

(AJP Taylor *The Origins of the Second World War* Penguin 1964. pp 133-134)

5 THE SPANISH CIVIL WAR

The Civil War which erupted in Spain in July 1936 was quickly seen by the rest of Europe as a struggle between the aggressive and advancing creed of Fascism and the waning force of democracy. The Spaniards did not necessarily see their war in these terms, but that mattered little to the rest of the continent which rapidly became embroiled.

The Rise and Fall of the Spanish Empire

How was it that the unfortunate Spanish people found themselves in this mess? By 1990 Spain was a prosperous member of the European Community and was led by an apparently stable democratic government. In the 16th century she was the world's strongest power. In the period between Spain has had its problems. While their Portuguese neighbours pioneered the sea route to India in the years leading up to 1500, the Spanish helped themselves to most of South and Central America. Today Brazil, where Portuguese is the dominant language, is the only country in that continent where Spanish is not the national language. The Spanish imposed the Catholic religion on their colonies and at the same time they exploited them ruthlessly, extracting fabulous wealth. This was probably the beginning of their decline because the huge amounts of gold they imported destroyed the value of their own gold coinage by causing impressive inflation which left their economy permanently weakened.

In the 16th century Spain took on the role of the Pope's champion in the fight against the Protestant reformation. The defeat of the Spanish Armada by the English weather in 1588 is only one of many tales of failure which strained and weakened an ailing society.

By the early 19th century Spain had truly become a third-rate power. In 1808 she was conquered, briefly, by her erstwhile ally, France, under Napoleon, whose brother, Joseph, became King. Joseph attempted to introduce new liberal ideas to Spain, restricting the power of the church and the landowners and trying to modernise the country's economy, but the Spanish, naturally, did not relish foreign rule. Once Napoleon himself had left Spain they rebelled and, assisted by British forces led by the Duke of Wellington, ejected the French.

19th Century Liberal Reforms :
An Increasingly Divided Nation

Despite their association with foreign influences the liberals were able, with help from the army, to overthrow the unpopular King Ferdinand in 1820 and introduce a democratic constitution. They also attacked the wealth and power of the Catholic Church, which was recognised as the 'sole religion of Spain', but which was stripped of most of its land. The liberals intended to deal with rural poverty by selling the Church's land to peasants, but most of it found its way into the possession of already rich landowners, thus exaggerating a growing gulf between rich and poor in rural Spain. Devout Catholics were also distressed by the closing down of monasteries. These changes had the effect of making the Church even more reactionary. It longed for a strong, authoritarian Catholic King who would restore its wealth and influence and to this end increasingly identified itself with the very rich - the only people who might be able to give it what it wanted.

Ferdinand was restored to power by the French but he was unable to grant all the Church's wishes. He died in 1833 without a male heir and passed the throne on to his wife and daughter. The Salic Law demanded a male monarch and the more traditional elements in Spain supported the claims of Ferdinand's brother Don Carlos, a man of very traditional views. The great contradiction in the Carlist's creed was that the Salic law was not traditionally Spanish but had been imported from France. However, Carlist revolts broke out immediately. Priests fought for the cause and nuns made cartridges for their guns. Most Carlists were conservative peasants from the hill areas of the north. The revolt developed into a civil war which did not end until 1839 when the army took effective control of the country. Sometimes army rulers espoused liberal ideas, but more often they were traditionalists and the church was able to partially restore its position.

In order to control the increasingly restive peasantry the 'Civil Guard' was created in 1844. Their original task was bandit control but they quickly became symbols of oppression. Two men, always from another part of Spain, were stationed in each village. They lived in fortified houses and were forbidden to make social contact with the villagers, who came to hate their green uniforms and three-cornered hats.

Army rule continued until 1868 when a messy revolution broke out. For a time Spain became a republic, before the monarchy was restored under Alphonso XII , a King controlled by rich landowners.

During these domestic difficulties Spain lost most of her Empire. Her major South American colonies declared themselves independent in 1821 and in 1898 the USA assisted the Cubans and Philippinos to eject their Spanish

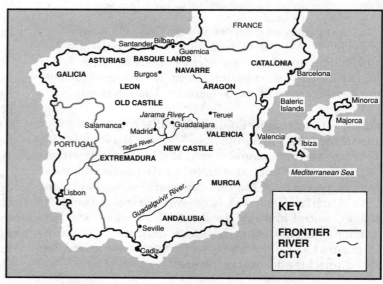

The provinces of Spain, 1936

masters. A long-running and brutal conflict broke out in Spanish Morocco between the Riffs and the Spanish army.

It has been said of post war Britain that she has lost an Empire and has yet to find a role. Britain's economic failings are sometimes attributed to loss of self-confidence. We felt our Empire had something good to offer its subject people and when they rejected it and demanded independence our self-belief collapsed and all sorts of national failures resulted. By 1936 the Spanish had been suffering this problem for over a century and it had gone a long way towards destroying their national pride.

Economic Problems

Spain was also an economic failure. Little industrialisation occurred outside the Basque provinces, where the steel industry was centred on Bilbao, and Catalonia , where the port of Barcelona was the home of a strong textiles industry.

Primitive Agriculture : Braceros and Latifundias.

Throughout the rest of Spain, the vast majority of people lived in conditions of grinding poverty, which stood in stark contrast to the wealth of the few rich, landowning families whose oppulent lifestyle depended on their 'latifundias', huge estates where primitive agriculture was practised. Conditions varied from province to province but things were probably worst in Andalusia where much of the land was under-utilised and where there were large numbers of landless 'braceros', agricultural workers who depended on casual labour on the latifundias and who frequently starved in unemployment. It is estimated that there were about 2.5 million braceros in Spain in 1930.

Political Divisions and Extremism

Anarchism

This maldistribution of wealth polarised Spanish society. The poor came to favour violent and radical change. Many became anarchists, followers of the 19th century Russian thinker Mikhail Bakunin. They believed that fairer distribution of wealth could only be achieved by destroying all authority. Since the Church and the army consistently sided with the landowners this attitude is understandable. Only in the Basque country were priests seen to be the friends of the labouring poor and respected by them. The anarchists were opposed to large-scale centralised government such as exists in every European state today. They wanted society to be organised on the basis of small-scale local communes in which everybody participates in decision making. Their urge to destroy the existing order led to the assassinations and bank robberies for which they were renowned. In 1906 they tried to blow up the King on his wedding day.

Syndicalism

In the towns anarchism took the form of 'syndicalist' trade unions (syndicalist is taken from the French word for a trade union) . The idea of 'anarcho-syndicalism' was that trade union power, expressed through strikes, could be used to destroy the power of the state. Eventually the anarchist unions merged to form the Confederation Nacional del Trabajo (CNT) in 1911.

The Marxists

Rivals for the hearts and minds of the town workers were the socialists and marxists, who believed in the state ownership of the means of producing wealth (farms, factories, shops etc.) In contrast to the anarchists, they believed in centralised state power. Their Union General de Trabajadores (UGT) sometimes sank its differences with the syndicalists and joined their strikes. Socialism was strongest in Madrid and the surrounding province of Castille. Elsewhere in Spain the main challenge to authority came from the anarchists, Barcelona being the great stronghold of the CNT.

Regional Separatists

Religion and politics were not the only divisive forces in Spain. The country was also bedevilled by demands for regional autonomy. Its many regions all had their own distinctive customs and spoke different dialects. Most regions resented the supremacy of Madrid and Castille, none more than the Basques and Catalans whose languages are totally different from Castillian Spanish. Even today ETA continues to grab headlines in its violent struggle for Basque home rule. Other provinces, such as Asturias and Andalusia, had definite separatist tendencies. Even in the disaffected provinces, however, there were divisions. There were many Carlists among the peasants of the hill areas of the Basque Provinces. In the great civil war their Requetés (volunteers) fought for the old Spanish establishment against the separatists and the socialist government.

It can therefore be said, without fear of contradiction, that Spain was a divided country. The establishment was generally supported by and consisted of the landowners, the Church, the army, monarchists and Carlists. The enemies of the establishment, all seeking change in different ways, were peasants and town workers, anarchists, socialists, communists, Basque and Catalan separatists, republicans and liberals. Perhaps the most surprising thing about civil war in Spain was that it did not happen more often.

The Dictatorship of Primo de Rivera

By the late 19th and early 20th centuries Spain had a corrupt and inefficient system of elected government. The years 1918-1923 were a time of total chaos. In five years Spain had twelve governments, each of which failed to make any impact on the intense economic difficulties of that era. In 1923 military dictatorship was established under General Miguel Primo de Rivera, a man of energy and some imagination, who addressed himself with vigour to the formidable task of sorting out the mess.

With French military help de Rivera crushed the long-running revolt in Morocco and ended the terrible drain on Spanish lives and money in that colony. He worked hard to improve law and order and to improve the economy. The outdated railway system was re-equipped, the telephone network was improved, new roads were built and old ones widened or repaired and food production was increased by the introduction of irrigation to dry areas. Unfortunately the thorny question of land reform was ignored. Rivera was intolerant of criticism or dissent- he probably had to be to survive. Trade unions were largely unaffected but he suppressed the Cortes

(Parliament), City Councils and political parties and censored the press.

Rivera gave Spain seven years of relative stability and progress but the King never liked him. The world economic collapse of 1929 created a very difficult situation. The army turned against him too and in 1930 he went into exile. With the situation getting out of hand elections for the Municipal (City) Councils were held. The results showed the King, Alfonso XIII, to be extremely unpopular. He abdicated and followed Rivera into exile in 1931. For the second time in her history Spain was a Republic.

The Azana Reforms

The new Republic inherited all the old Spanish problems and the great depression. A moderate Socialist government took office under Manuel Azana and initiated a series of reforms which achieved little but served to agitate all groups in Spanish society.

Land Reform
Azana's Government addressed itself to the thorny question of land reform. A policy of breaking up the latifundia and transferring the land to peasant communes or individual owners was introduced but achieved little apart from

upsetting the landowners and frustrating the braceros. The law applied, initially, to only a few provinces and few estates were broken up as there wasn't enough money available to compensate dispossessed landowners. Nevertheless, the rich felt that they were faced with revolution while the peasants, whose hopes had been aroused, continued to starve.

A More Efficient Army
The army also needed attention. It had far too many officers, many of whom were too old or fat to do their work. Many of the more hopeless cases were generously pensioned off. They had no grounds to complain about their treatment and the army was left in the charge of the 'Africanistas', tough professional soldiers, like General Francisco Franco, who had learned their trade fighting the Riffs in Morocco. Unfortunately for the government, these men had their own ideas about how the country should be run and they were not in the least like Azana's.

The Church Further Alienated
Azana's regime also tackled the problem of Church and state. The government stopped paying priests and the Church lost control of state schools, although it was still allowed to run its own. The Catholic Church has always

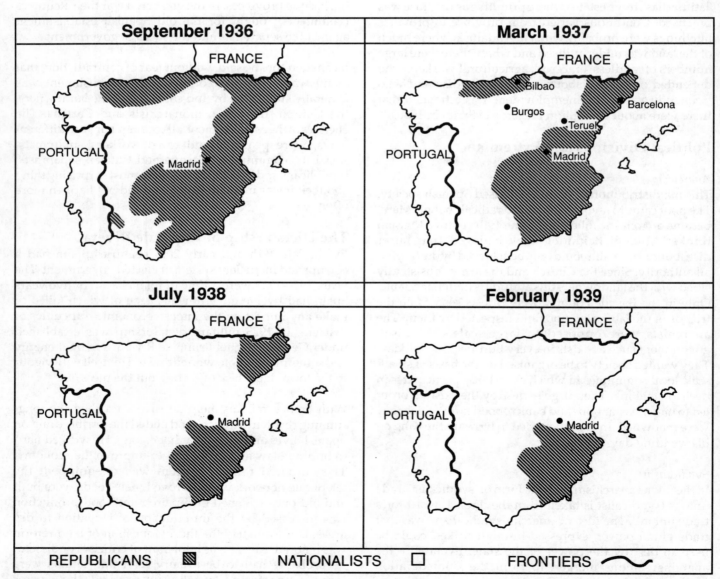

The progress of the civil war in Spain, 1936-39

attached great importance to education as a way of influencing the morals and behaviour of the young, so these changes confirmed its suspicions of the Republic.

The Falange Española : Spanish Fascism

Fascism had reared its ugly head in most European countries at this time and it is not surprising that Spain was no exception. In 1933 José Antonio Rivera, son of the old dictator, founded the Falange Española which soon incorporated another neo-fascist group, JONS. The Falange was not a carbon copy of Italy's Fascist party or of Germany's Nazis, but it had certain similarities. It was anti-parliamentary and sought one party rule. Naturally the Falange would be the ruling party. It wasn't racist but it did talk a lot about Spain's mission in the world and attached great importance to loyalty and obedience to the Roman Catholic Church. The Falange was quick to copy the private army tactics of Hitler's SA and Mussolini's Blackshirts.

Elections were held in 1934 and the Conservative Government which came to power under Lerroux ignored or reversed the Azana reforms, dashing the hope of the poor, the powerless and the dispossessed.

Popular Fronts : Alliances of the Left

At this point events outside Spain began to play an important role in her domestic politics. For many years the Moscow government had forbidden European Communist parties to co-operate with moderate socialists. This policy made them isolated and weak so in the early thirties Stalin reversed it. A number of Popular Front Alliances were created which included revolutionaries like the communists as well as reforming parties. A Popular Front government came to power in France under the moderate Socialist, Leon Blum, and, in February 1936, elections in Spain returned an alliance of Republicans, Socialists and Communists. This was the spark which lit the fires of civil war in Spain.

THE WAR

Rightwing backlash against the Popular Front

The ministers of the Popular Front Government elected in February 1936 were all moderates - there were no Communists. However, the right reacted violently and resorted to terrorism which provoked the Communists to do the same. Judges who condemned Falangists or journalists who criticised them were assassinated. Gangs with machine guns roamed the streets of Madrid gunning down their opponents.

The groups that took advantage of this civil unrest were the army officers, traditionalists and monarchists led by Calvo Sotelo, who had been Minister of Finance under de Rivera. When Sotelo was murdered on 13 July 1936, General Sanjurjo led an army revolt in Spanish Morocco. The next day army officers in almost every garrison in Spain rose in support. Sanjurjo had been sentenced to death for his role in a coup attempt in 1932 but he had been reprieved. However, at this stage he was killed in a plane crash and was replaced by General Francisco Franco. This was

essentially a revolt of army officers. These risings had become such an established part of Spain's political tradition that they even had a name. An officer revolt was called a 'pronunciamento'. In his pronunciamento Franco was supported by the Falange. They hoped to stage a coup d'état, not to start a civil war. They were unable to seize power quickly for the following reasons:

1 The mass of the Spanish people resisted the revolt and fought it for three years.

2 Foreign powers saw it as a struggle between Fascism and democracy or Socialism and intervened until the point of exhaustion was reached.

3 The two sides were finely balanced in term of resources.

Republicans V Nationalists

On paper the initial advantages lay with the rebels, or 'Nationalists'. They had the advantages of surprise, superior military strength and greater experience of fighting. Many army officers had fought in Morocco and the Falangists were already well equipped.

The navy, however, was divided. Each side had one battleship and since most of the rebel forces were in Morocco they could not take rapid advantage of their strength. Naval officers were Nationalists but the ordinary sailors were Republicans, supporters of the democratically elected Popular Front Government.

The Republican side consisted of a few army officers, notably Generals Miaja and Rojo , a mass of workers and peasants trained in military service and most Basques and Catalans. They held important economic resources in the industrial areas of Madrid and Barcelona as well as some of the richest farming areas.

By the end of 1936 the Nationalists held rather more than half of Spain, mostly in the south, west and northwest and the Balearic Isles. Franco proclaimed himself to be the "Chief of the Spanish State" at the head of a "Nationalist Government", whose headquarters were at Burgos.

The Republican Government, which moved to Valencia eventually, was led by the Socialist Largo Caballero. It held all eastern and southeastern Spain, Madrid and most of the northern coastal belt. If there had been no foreign intervention it seems likely that the Republicans would have won in the end as they had the bulk of the population and important agricultural and industrial resources on their side.

From the beginning both sides fought with the utmost ferocity and atrocities were common. Both sides shot prisoners. The Republicans often shot priests, except in the Basque country, and Civil Guards. *[See Sources 10 and 13]* On one occasion an entire village turned up to shoot a captured officer. They all fired their rifles at him until his body was reduced to an unrecognisable pulp. As in all civil wars, even families found themselves divided and fought among themselves. The nature of the war was recognised by Schwendemann, a German official. In a memorandum to Berlin in 1938 he wrote,

"A compromise between the fighting parties appears impossible, above all for ideological reasons, but also because so much unjustly shed blood has flowed between the two ... Only a radical victory of one of the two parties appears thinkable, with the consequence that the leader stratum of the losing side will be eliminated down to the leaders of middle and lower rank, either by flight abroad or by execution after more or less summary proceedings. At any rate that is what has happened in the areas so far conquered by Franco."

(*Documents in German Foreign Policy. Series D. Vol 3*)

In Republican areas the army rising set off a spontaneous revolution which often threatened to divert popular attention away from the task of winning the war. In Madrid the socialist trade union UGT was in the driving seat, in the countryside it was the anarchists while in Barcelona an uneasy coalition of anarchists, socialists and communists formed an Anti-Fascist Committee. Workers took over factories, cafes and shops were collectivised, churches were closed down or burned and marriages took place without a priest. Middle-class people kept out of sight or went unshaven and hatless in old clothes to avoid identification. In the countryside land was redistributed and churches became barns or byres. The military had precipitated the revolution which they claimed they were acting to prevent.

Foreign Intervention

The biggest problem facing the Nationalists at the outset was transporting their forces from Morocco. On 27th July 1936 the German Foreign Ministry received a telegram from its embassy in Lisbon, Portugal .

"The following concrete proposals have now been received from the Provisional Government at Burgos : Appealing to our common anti-communist interest, we request the earliest possible delivery to Saragossa or Burgos of at least ten Junker transports, and , if possible up to twenty bombers also..."

(*Documents in German Foreign Policy*. Series D Vol. 3, Doc 12.)

Germany helpfully provided thirty Junker transport planes which literally kept Franco's forces in the war in the early stages. In November 1936 Germany and Italy officially recognised Franco's regime and clearly expected a rapid victory.

In the New Year, General Miaja organised the Republican's defence of Madrid, and among the reinforcements sent to him was the first of the International Brigades. *[See Source 11]* These were recruited from left-wing oppponents of Fascism in several European countries, including France and Britain, as well as from the ranks of anti-Fascists in Italy and Germany. Some of these volunteers had fought in the Great War but the majority had no military training. They included workers and trade unionists, students, adventurers and writers like Ernest Hemingway and George Orwell. Many were Communists. They were bound together by a passionate belief that Fascism had gone too far and had to be stopped in Spain. They gave up their jobs, if they had any, and made their way to Paris at their own expense. From there they were sent on to Spain by an organisation run by Josip Broz, who later ruled Yugoslavia as Marshall Tito.

Unit names indicate something of the Brigades' ideology. The Germans fought in the Thaelmann Brigade, named in honour of the leader of the German Communist Party, outlawed by Hitler. Many Americans served in the Abraham Lincoln Brigade, while the anti-Fascist Italians formed the Garibaldi Brigade. The latter was called after the great 19th century liberal, Giuseppe Garibaldi, who learned his trade as a freedom fighter in South America before leading 'the thousand' , 'the Redshirts', in a crusade which overthrew the corrupt and despotic Bourbon monarchy in Southern Italy and made possible the unification of Italy in 1870. Garibaldi was one of the most romantic and charismatic figures in European History and had he lived in the 1930s it is not hard to imagine that his huge bearded figure would have been seen in a flaming red shirt leading the brigade in the fight for freedom in Spain.

Towards the end of 1938 the Brigades withdrew because of a League of Nations peace initiative. By that time about 40,000 volunteers had fought in the Brigades although there had never been more than 15,000 at any time; 2,300 had gone from Britain, most serving in the 15th Brigade. About 500 men went from Scotland, half of these coming from Glasgow. 123 went from Dundee of whom 17 were killed. About 60% of the Glasgow men were Communist Party members and 20% belonged to the Labour Party. These figures were reflected in British recruitment as a whole. About 540 British volunteers were killed including John Cornford, a talented young poet and a Communist.

Garry McCartney recalled how he came to be involved:

"In the summer of 1936 Bill Donaldson and I were in Skye climbing the Cuillins. We had been there since the beginning of the Glasgow Fair ... When we came down from the hill we learned that there was a war raging in Spain.
Now Bill and I were both in the Communist Party. It didn't take us very long to come to a decision that rather than just speak about being anti-Fascist, here was an opportunity of doing something much more tangible. We agreed that we should consider seriously the whole question of getting to Spain to play our part.

We were already politically motivated, as were many, many thousands of people up and down the country, because we had seen the advent of Fascism in Germany in 1933, when Hitler got in power. We had seen Mussolini flexing his muscles in the Abyssinian war. So Fascism was on the march in Europe. And in Britain Mosley, who had made attempts to form his New Party by coming to the St Andrews Halls in Glasgow for a meeting ... of the British Union of Fascists. Actually Mosley was the party.
The working-class movement in Glasgow was very much informed and very much involved in the anti-Fascist struggle... Bill and I were both working and made overtures to the Party to get to Spain."

Another volunteer, David Stirrat, commented:

"At the time I felt I had a duty to go and do something about it ... I'm not particularly keen on being a soldier because I think it's alien to my nature. Some people like that kind of thing, you know, but it's not the kind of thing I would choose. But sometimes we do things that we think we ought to do."

John Dunlop recalled that not all volunteers were like David Stirrat and that some felt uncomfortable about the Communist domination of the Brigades.

"I don't think Barney Shields was a member of any political party. He was just anti-Fascist. He had come to Spain because, I suppose like a lot of Glasgow fellows, he was a fighting man and he wanted to get in and have a fight on the right side. I think the fact that he didn't like the commissars was an indication of his non-alignment with any political party. The commissars were the creation of the Russian Communists... But Barney didn't feel that he needed any political instruction on what he was there to do. He regarded political commissars - I think rather unfairly - as more or less non-combatant busybodies."
"... I think Barney was a bit unfair to Wally Tapsell (a commissar), because Wally, like Barney, died a hero's death in the retreat back from Aragon in the spring of 1938 ..."

Throughout the War the Republican side was urged on by the fiery, inspirational speeches of La Pasionaria, Delores Ibarruri, one of the two Communists in the Government. Tommy Bloomfield, a Scot, remembered her speech of thanks to the Brigades before they were withdrawn.

"Goodbye, my sons. Come back to us. You have made history. You are a legend."

(The four preceding extracts are from *Voices from the Spanish Civil War* edited by Ian MacDougall)

Throughout the non-Fascist world, collections were organised to send humanitarian aid to Republican Spain. The Labour Party, the TUC, the Communists, the Co-operative Movement and others collected money, food and clothes to send to Spain. A Scottish Ambulance Unit consisting of 6 motor ambulances and 20 staff drove out to Spain to relieve the suffering close behind the Republican lines.

The Soviet Union also sent fighter planes to the Republicans to balance the assistance the rebels were getting from Germany and Italy. Italy sent whole regiments of its army who had 'volunteered' to fight in Spain.

The Battle for Madrid - Winter 1936-37
In November 1936 Franco's forces pushed their way up to the western outskirts of Madrid, but failed to capture the city. They then tried to move north, as the first stage of an encircling plan, but in February the Nationalists' crack Moorish troops and Foreign Legion were held up at *Jarama* by Spanish Communists and French, British and American International Brigades. Casualties were appalling - the French were wiped out - but Madrid still held. The American Brigade won their new battle song - to the tune of 'Red River Valley.'

"There's a place in Spain called Jarama
It's a place that we all know too well

For 'tis there that we wasted our manhood
And most of our old age as well."

Sixteen Glasgow men died at Jarama. The following month the Nationalists were back with 35,000 Italian 'volunteers' equipped with tanks, artillery and aircraft. At *Guadalajara*, to the northeast of Madrid, they were delayed by snow. Spanish Communists and the International Brigades moved into the attack, backed by tanks and aircraft supplied by the Russians. Italians in the International Brigades fought their Fascist countrymen who staged one of the lightning retreats for which they were to become famous. Madrid had been saved, for the time being, and the Brigades had proved that a makeshift army with little training but with determination and a willingness to die for their cause can defeat professionals who lack commitment. Mussolini was furious.

Guernica and the Fall of the Basque Lands - Summer 1937
After Gualalajara, Franco decided to turn his attention to the north in order to eliminate the Basque enclave. By midsummer of 1937 Bilbao, the Basque capital, had been captured. The Basques had resisted stoutly at first but they crumbled after the horrific bombing of *Guernica* by the German Condor Legion. The town was first bombed with high explosives, then with fire bombs, before the fugitives were machine gunned from the air. As is often the case when towns are bombed, the main targets, a bridge and an arms factory were left intact as was the tree of Guernica, an ancient meeting place and symbol of Basque liberties. Responsibility for this act seems to lie with the German commander in the area. The Nationalists later claimed that the Basques fired the town themselves to deny its use to their enemies. However, throughout the war the Basques had distinguished themselves by abstaining from atrocities. The victorious Nationalists proceeded to shoot as many Republican leaders as they could lay their hands on. The Basque language was suppressed and Castillian culture imposed. It is not surprising that many Basques today are still unreconciled to Spain and that ETA is so violent. Picasso's painting 'Guernica' gives some impression of the horror of the event. *[See Sources 12A and 12B]*

In May 1937 Caballero was replaced by Don Juan Negrin, a more moderate Socialist, and, by the end of the year, thanks to general conscription , he commanded a force of some eight hundred thousand men. In October the government moved to Barcelona in loyal Catalonia and in December it defeated the Nationalists at Teruel, where rebel advances threatened to cut government-held territory in two. The situation at the end of 1937 was one of stalemate as each side had consolidated its defensive position. For this reason the extent of foreign help became decisive.

France and Britain - The Policy of Non-Intervention.
Aid reached the Nationalists through Portugal where Salazar, the dictator, was keen to help. Aid reached the Republicans through France, where the Popular Front Government of Leon Blum was sympathetic but scared to be seen doing too much in case it provoked a right-wing backlash in France, thereby risking its own programme of reforms. Michael Foot claims that Blum intended to help

the Republicans until Baldwin's British Goverment made it clear that they would not help him against Germany, as promised in the Locarno pact, if he were to do so. Terrified of Germany, Blum acquiesced.

Leon Blum was reluctant to leave another Popular Front Government in the lurch, so he suggested to the British that a policy of non-intervention by all European powers should be promoted. The British seized on this with enthusiasm and referred to it thereafter as an idea which the French had come up with on their own. While the Republican Government of Spain was persuaded not to appeal to the League, Britain took the initiatve in setting up a 'Non-Intervention Committee' whose members included Britain, France, Italy, Germany and Russia. The Republicans thought that they could win the war if foreign powers could be persuaded to stay out and so accepted this at first.

British Attitudes to the War

Baldwin's largely Conservative Government thought that Franco was going to win the war and they did not want to make an enemy of him, nor did they want to further antagonise Mussolini.The conservative British establishment was also very suspicious of Republican Spain, which it saw as Communist rather than democratic. Many Conservatives sympathised with Franco's stance against trade unions and government policies to improve the lot of Spain's poor. Many International Brigaders saw non-intervention as a Tory conspiracy to destroy the Republic.

After Guernica the British government became obsessed by the image of the flaming town and were increasingly reluctant to contemplate any sort of war. "The bomber will always get through", they said. "If London is bombed, the dead will number hundreds of thousands." The right wing of the Labour Party accepted this and supported non-intervention. The left wing, especially Nye Bevan and Manny Shinwell, saw that non-intervention in fact meant preventing the legitimate government of Spain, as recognised by the League of Nations, from getting supplies, while the rebels were being illegally supplied and helped by the Fascist powers. Britain and France were losing a chance to stop the "advance of Fascism". To the left, German and Italian intervention was aggression against a sovereign, democratically elected government. The Labour left began to drift away from pacifism and many fought in the International Brigades.

The Labour Party was further divided along religious lines. Throughout Europe the Roman Catholic Church supported the Nationalists against the allegedly godless, priest murdering Republicans. A special Irish Force, led by O'Duffy, fought for Franco with the blessing of the Irish Catholic Church. The majority of Scottish Catholics were poor, often of Irish descent, and generally supported Labour. The Civil War divided them. While some fought in the International Brigades, others collected money for the Nationalists or signed petitions,

"I protest against the organised slaughter of Christians and the destruction of property in Spain by Communists who have by force usurped the place of the elected representatives of the Spanish people. I call upon His Majesty's Government to use its influence for the protection of the Spanish patriots who are fighting for civil and religious liberty against a Communistic dictatorship which is a threat to the peace and stability of the British Empire."
(From *The Catholic Herald and Glasgow Observer*, 12 Sept. 1936)

The League of Nations

When the war was discussed by the League, the Republicans claimed that non-intervention was illegal since it denied help to a government recognised by the League, while failing to stop German and Italian aggression against that government. By this time, however, the League had come to be recognised as a spent force. None of the major powers even pretended to operate through it.

The Nyon Conference.

The 'Non-intervention Committee' set up a naval blockade to stop weapons getting into Spain but it was utterly ineffective. 'Mystery' submarines began to sink ships taking supplies to the Republic and in August 1937 a British destroyer reported a torpedo attack on her. In the same month two Italian destroyers had shadowed a Spanish oil tanker, the *Campeador*, all day. She was attacked at night with torpedoes and shells and her crew were left struggling in water ablaze with oil. Entries in the diary of Italy's Foreign Minister, Count Ciano, belatedly confirm who was responsible for these events.

"31st August 1937 : The naval blockade is producing striking results: four Russian or Red steamers sunk, one Greek captured, one Spanish shelled and obliged to take refuge in a French Port ..."
September 2nd : The navy is very active - three torpedoings and one prize. But international opinion is getting worked up. Particularly in England, as a result of the attack on the destroyer *Havock*, fortunately not hit. It was the *Iride* (Italian submarine). The row has already started."
(*Ciano's Diary. 1937-38.* Translated by A Mayor pp 7-8)

Britain called for a conference at Nyon near Geneva to discuss the matter. Germany and Italy did not attend but the British and French Navies were ordered to destroy submarines or aircraft attacking non-Spanish ships in the Mediterranean. The piracy came to a sudden end but the lesson that it pays to be firm with Fascists was not learned. The Republicans asked that protection be extended to Spanish ships but this was not accepted.

Soviet Attitudes to the War

Stalin provided the Republicans with just enough aid to keep them going. He knew that Britain and France would not tolerate a communist government in Spain so he could not win the war. However, he liked to see the German and Italian forces kept busy in Spain, where they could not attack Russia, so he tried to make the war last as long as possible.

Nazi Germany's Attitude

Speaking at a Nazi Party rally at Nuremberg in 1937 Hitler said:

"As you know, in Spain this Jewish Bolshevism has advanced by a roundabout way through democracy to open revolution. It is a gross perversion of the facts to maintain that the Bolshevist oppressors of the people in that country are the representatives of legal authority, while the fighters of Nationalist Spain are illegal revolutionaries... Can we remain neutral in the face of such happenings as these?"

(Norman Baynes (ed) *The Speeches of Adolf Hitler* p.702)

Hitler used the Spanish war as a testing ground for his air force. The Condor Legion gave help with air transport and its dive bombers obliterated ground targets like Guernica. The Hossbach Memorandum (see page**XX**) also reveals that Hitler was happy to see Italy tied up in Spain so that Germany was free to act in Austria. German Foreign Ministry archives captured after the Second World War show that the Germans were keen to secure supplies of iron ore and other vital materials of war from Spain. Franco was well aware of this and made sure that the Germans got little for nothing.

Fascist Italy's Motives

Mussolini hoped to establish the Mediterranean as an Italian sphere of influence ('Mare Nostrum') and he probably had designs on the Balearic Isles. He hoped that war in Spain would prove to be more effective in hardening the Italian national character than the Abyssinian adventure. Both Hitler and Mussolini probably felt an ideological bond with Franco since all espoused right - wing authoritarian ideas. Count Ciano, who was married to Mussolini's daughter, Edda, wrote in his diary on 29th October 1937:

"I examined my conscience and asked whether this blood had been shed in a good cause. Yes, the answer is yes. At Malaga, at Guadalajara, at Santander, we are fighting in defence of our civilisation and our revolution. And sacrifices are necessary in order to forge the bold and strong spirit of a nation."

(*Ciano Diaries 1937-1938* edited A Mayor p. 26 in *Italy under Mussolini*.)

The End of the War

By the spring of 1938, Franco, backed by as many as 100,000 Italians and good German equipment, was strong enough to renew his advance. The Government forces, short of equipment despite Russian help, were torn by dissension from within. The Republican 'militias' were made up of units which reflected their political leanings. Thus there were anarchist units, marxists, trade unionists, Asturian miners, Catalan separatists etc. They fought the Nationalists and quarrelled among themselves with passionate bravery. Few saw any need for military discipline. They might spend hours debating whether to obey an order or not. Naturally they avoided drill and saluting. A sentry, convinced that there was 'nothing doing', might go off into town to see his girl, intending to return when he was really needed.

Teruel

In order to draw Franco's forces away from Madrid, the Republicans had attacked and captured the lightly defended town of Teruel in December 1937. The Nationalists rose to the bait and three months of fierce fighting took place in bitterly cold winter weather.

In February 1938 the rebels took Teruel. Driving eastwards to the sea, they cut Government territory in half.

Barcelona and Madrid, despite heavy and repeated bombing, held out until early 1939. Barcelona fell at the end of January and Madrid at the end of March. Many thousands of Spaniards fled to France to escape the reprisals which Franco proceeded to take against his opponents. Spain lapsed into the peace of exhaustion as foreigners withdrew.

The Cost of the War

The Civil War probably cost Spain one million dead as well as the destuction of her cities and the laying waste of much of her countryside. Franco established himself in power where he long survived his sponsors, Hitler and Mussolini, being in power until his death in 1975.

Consequences of Franco's Victory

1 Franco's victory was another triumph for Hitler. He had again defeated Britain and France in that he had ignored non-intervention, which was also the policy of the League, and had continued to support Franco. Democracy had again been discredited and authoritarian Fascism appeared triumphant.

2 Hitler was also pleased to have another potential ally on France's southern frontier, almost completing her encirclement. However Spain had limited value as an ally. Exhausted by the Civil War she remained neutral in the Second World War.

3 The Rome-Berlin Axis was seen to be a reality. Italy and Germany had shown that they could and would work together in pursuit of a policy of aggressive nationalism. The Stresa Front idea of detaching the less menacing Mussolini from Hitler now seemed hopeless.

4 National opinion in the democracies (UK, France, USA) was divided by the war. (See page 32 on the effects on the British Labour and Conservative parties.) Vast differences of opinion existed as to how the 'Fascist Menace' should be dealt with.

5 The outcome of the war was less ominous for Europe than many people feared. The war was never, as many people claimed, a war between Communism and Fascism. It was a clash between all the forces in Spain which believed in democratic, Republican government and social reform and all the forces which clung to the old order. The victorious, Nationalist government stayed neutral in the Second World War and did not join in a European Fascist crusade. It was purely a reactionary Spanish government concerned only with Spanish affairs. Schwendemann, a German official in Spain, recognised this when he wrote:

"It is actually a life and death struggle between the two Spains : nationalist, traditional, agrarian, monarchist, Catholic-clerical Spain, which is now strongly oriented towards a social programme... through the influence of the Falange; and the Spain of the Liberals, Socialists, Communists, Anarchists, Freethinkers and Freemasons, which in some way stems from the French Revolution of 1789."

(*Documents in German Foreign Policy* Series D Vol.3)

Likewise, the Republican forces had never been predominantly Communist. The government had been a broad based affair and, although there were many Communists in the International Brigades, there were also many Liberals and moderate Socialists.

6 The weakness of appeasement, that is giving ground to the dictators in the hope that they would be satisfied and pacified, was again shown. The backing down of the Italians over the 'pirate submarine' incident showed what a firm stance could achieve. Sadly this lesson was not heeded. Britain was about to try and appease Hitler over Czechoslovakia.

7 The war provided and, proved to be, a testing ground for new weapons and tactics. Hitler and Mussolini cynically used it to give their forces, especially pilots, practice. The damage done to Spanish cities by these bombers accentuated fears among British politicians of such damage to British cities in event of a war with Germany. "The bomber will always get through". Strohrer, the German Ambassador in Spain, sent this perceptive comment home to his Foreign Ministry in March 1938.

"The Red Government is using the general indignation aroused by these air attacks to encourage the resistance and endurance of the population, who had been thrown into consternation by Franco's military successes in Aragon. As a sign that these bombing attacks did not result in an effective demoralisation of the population of Barcelona, it has been pointed out that many of the wounded, while being carried on stretchers to first aid posts and hospitals, exhorted the public with clenched fists and exclamations of hatred to carry on further resistance."

(*Documents in German Foreign Policy* Series D Vol 3)

The ability of aerial bombardment to destroy civilian morale is often overestimated. Ironically, at this time a brilliant Scotsman, Robert Watson-Watt, was perfecting a new invention called radar, while a clever English designer and engineer called Reginald Mitchell was building a fast little aeroplane with outstanding manoeuverability, a remarkable rate of climb and four Browning machine guns on each wing. It was to be called the Supermarine Spitfire. Both of these inventions were to shorten the odds on the bomber getting through or home. The bombers of Guernica would one day set fire to London, Glasgow, Coventry and other British towns but they would pay a high price for their achievements and they would not be able to bomb Britain into submission.

Franco ruled Spain with a rod of iron until his death in 1975. By that time Spain had developed a vigorous and expanding economy. The monarchy and parliamentary democracy were restored and appear firmly rooted and healthy. Republican exiles returned from France. Among these was La Pasionaria who was able to die in her homeland in 1990.

THE INCLINED PLANE?

After the Rhineland affair Hitler did his best to pour oil on the troubled waters of European diplomacy. On the day of remilitarisation he said, "Germany has no territorial claims to make in Europe". Subsequent events would prove how deceitful this was. He offered to rejoin the League of Nations if its Covenant could be separated from the terms of the Treaty of Versailles, and offered non-aggression pacts lasting twenty five years to both his western and eastern neighbours.

European attention then turned to the Spanish Civil War and, although Hitler sent the Condor Legion to help the Nationalists, he generally kept a low profile for almost the next two years.

Towards the end of 1937 conditions were right for Hitler to act again. German rearmament had accelerated after 1936, while Britain and France had done little in this field. Their reactions to the Abyssinian crisis and the Spanish Civil War had shown them to be uncertain in the face of aggression. Italy, Germany's enemy over Austria, was embroiled in Spain and in Russia Stalin had been wrecking his own army by savage purges of the officer corps. In May 1937 Neville Chamberlain had succeeded Stanley Baldwin as Prime Minister of Britain. Chamberlain had been a leading advocate of appeasement in the British cabinet. Now he would take every opportunity to put his ideas into practice.

Military Strength of the Main European Powers

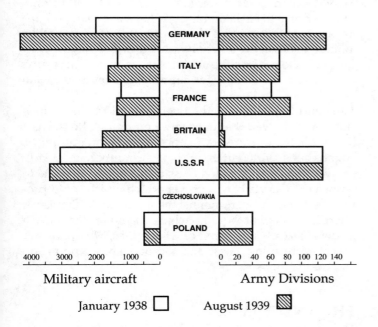

Military aircraft   Army Divisions

January 1938 ☐   August 1939 ▨

THE ASSUMPTIONS BEHIND APPEASEMENT

The policy of appeasement was based on a number of assumptions.

The Reasonable Nature of Germany's Demands
The most important assumption was that Germany had a limited number of reasonable demands which, when satisfied, would change her into a peaceful nation. These demands arose from the Treaty of Versailles about which the British had begun to feel guilty. Lord Lothian wrote to the *Manchester Guardian* on 9th May 1935:

> "National Socialism in its brutal aspects, both at home and abroad, is in considerable measure due to the fact that her neighbours were not able to make reasonable revisions in the treaties as war passions died down."
> (quoted in *Britain and Germany between the Wars* by Martin Gilbert p17)

Hitler could be trusted to keep his word
Hitler was seen as a reasonable man who could be trusted to keep his word. This view was reinforced by the impressions of leading politicians such as Phillip Kerr (Lord Lothian) and David Lloyd George who visited Germany in the thirties. In January 1935, after meeting Hitler, Lord Lothian wrote:

> "I am convinced that Hitler does not want war. I believe that what the Germans are after is a strong but not an excessive army which will enable them to deal with Russia...Hitler is anxious to come to terms with us and I think trusts us ... of course all the wolves of hatred and fear and suspicion are clamouring to prevent an understanding."
> (Unpublished letter *Lothian papers* quoted by Martin Gilbert in *Britain and Germany between the Wars* p99)

The Empire was not ready to fight
Chamberlain was the son of the great Victorian politician Joseph Chamberlain to whose ideas the British Empire had been central. Neville Chamberlain was appalled by the prospect of the British Empire having to fight a war against the Japanese in the Far East, the Italians in Africa and the Germans in Europe. He saw little prospect of help from America and at one stage, while Britain was still meant to be supporting the League's stance on Manchuria, proposed an Anglo-Japanese alliance regardless of opposition from the anti-Japanese Americans.

At the 1937 Imperial Prime Ministers' Conference, Chamberlain became aware that the majority of Dominion Prime Ministers were unwilling to give a firm commitment to resist Hitler. General Herzog of South Africa made it clear that he felt enough had not been done to rectify German grievances. Herzog was an Afrikaner and much has been made in recent years of the ideological sympathy which the more extreme nationalist elements among the Boers felt for Nazi racism. A legacy of anti-British feeling from the Boer War certainly still existed among the Afrikaner population of South Africa. Herzog was possibly influenced more by the views of the great liberal Afrikaner leader, Jan Christiaan Smuts. General Smuts had been in charge of South African forces during the First World War and had represented his country at Versailles where Herzog had assisted him. 'Slim Janie' (Smuts was not a thin man - 'slim' means sly in Afrikaans) objected to the whole atmosphere of the peace settlement from the beginning. He, and the great English economist, John Maynard Keynes, took the view that the treaty was much too severe on Germany and would cause trouble in the future. By the time Smuts had talked Lloyd George round to his point of view it was too late to change the treaty. In 1937 Herzog was merely saying to Chamberlain, "Janie told you this would happen". The South Africans hadn't forgotten how freely their blood had flowed at Delville Wood on the Somme and were not keen for this to happen again unless there was a very good reason for it.

The Australians and New Zealanders remembered how inept British leadership had cost them so dearly in Gallipoli and the Canadians had their memorials at Vimy Ridge and Beaumont Hamel to make them question exactly why they had been fighting a war in Europe, thousands of miles from home. The mood of the Dominion Prime Ministers was that Germany should not be needlessly provoked and that everything should be done to rectify existing grievances. Chamberlain must have reflected on the enormous contribution Empire forces had made to the allied war effort in the Great War and realised that British efforts to resist Hitler would be futile without them.

Britain had no reliable allies outwith the Empire
It was felt that Britain was so hopelessly isolated that she had no alternative to appeasement. When Chamberlain surveyed Britain's allies from the First World War, he saw that France was so divided in her internal politics that she could never be a reliable ally. He once said of her,

> "She can never keep a secret for more than half an hour or a government for more than nine months."

America had retreated into isolation; Russia had become Communist while Italy and Japan, under Fascist governments, had embarked on dangerous careers of aggression. Britain had no sound allies for a fight against Hitler.

The League did not offer a solution
Like other British and French leaders at this time, Chamberlain had little faith in the League of Nations as a body for resolving disputes. His instincts told him to get back to the old way of sorting out problems, face to face discussions between the leaders of the great powers. In time he would have to meet Hitler. A believer in old-fashioned power politics, rather than collective security, he nevertheless lacked experience in foreign affairs, having entered national politics late after a successful career as a reforming Lord Mayor of Birmingham.

Peace seeking statesmen often busy themselves trying to prevent the last war. Many people believe that the First World War was a totally unnecessary conflict which occurred because of a failure to establish dialogue between rival power blocks. Chamberlain was determined that this should not happen again and that he would talk to Hitler. With the wisdom of hindsight we can see that his policy was unlikely to have worked since Hitler was not the man Chamberlain hoped.

The economy was too weak for war
It was believed that the Great War and the great Depression had done so much damage to the British economy that it could not sustain war against the European dictatorships whose propaganda about economic achievements was sometimes too readily believed.

The armed forces were unprepared
Sir Samuel Hoare, who became Foreign Secretary in 1935, wrote,

> " The divisions that I found at the Foreign Office ... were the result of the general feeling of frustration, created by the repeated failure of a foreign policy without adequate force to support it...
> Vansittart (permanent under secretary at the FO) felt intensely this atmosphere of division and failure. It was his mission to dissipate it... Vansittart's refrain never ceased to ring in my head. 'We are terribly weak. We must gain time for becoming stronger. Only military strength will stop Hitler, and at present we do not possess it.' "
> (*Nine Troubled Years* by Viscount Templewood [Sir S Hoare] p138)

It was hoped that appeasement might help to buy time for rearmament.

The British people were unwilling to fight
The horrors of the Great War were still fresh in the minds of politicians and voters. In the East Fulham bye-election in 1933 a Conservative candidate favouring rearmament saw his 3,000 majority turn into a majority of 7,000 for his Labour pacifist opponent. The Baldwin Government saw this as an indication of strong pacifist sentiments among the electors even though the candidate, John Wilmot, had advocated reliance on a strong League of Nations rather than pure pacifism and had won many votes by campaigning on the housing issue. In a famous debate in the Oxford Union the privileged youth of that great University carried the motion that *This House would not fight for King and Country.*

Communism was the main threat to Britain and Europe
In 1934 David Lloyd George, Britain's last Liberal Prime Minister, said to Parliament, "...perhaps in a year, perhaps in two, the conservative elements in this country will be looking to Germany as a bulwark against communism in Europe ... Do not let us be in a hurry to condemn Germany. We shall be welcoming Germany as our friend." (Hansard)

Time and time again in the twenties and thirties British statesmen showed that they saw Communist Russia as a bigger threat to European peace than Germany. In his negotiations with Hitler in 1938, Chamberlain clearly showed that he distrusted Russia and hoped to come to terms with Germany as a power which which could provide "a strong bulwark against the spread of Bolshevism". There is a school of thought which maintains that British leaders basically approved of what Hitler, Mussolini and Franco were doing. These dictators attacked Communism and trade unions.

THE ANSCHLUSS
The agreement, made in October 1936, betweenGermany and Italy to respect the independence of Austria did not remain Hitler's policy for long. He was alarmed by British attempts to woo Mussolini, which resulted in an Anglo-Italian agreement in January 1937 to maintain the status quo in the Mediterranean. Göring was sent immediately to Rome, where he upset Mussolini by raising the Austrian question again.

In July 1936, two years after the unsuccessful attempt to take over Austria, an Austro-German agreement had been signed. Its published terms were as follows:

1 Germany re-affirmed her recognition of Austria's independence;
2 both powers agreed not to interfere in each other's internal affairs;
3 Austria would conduct a foreign policy consistent with her being a 'German State'.

There were also a number of secret clauses, the most important of which bound Austria to give prominent neo-Nazis, like Glaise-Horstenau and Seyss-Inquart a share in political responsibility.

Mussolini was keen that all existing agreements on Austria should be honoured, but when he received a conducted tour of Germany from the Führer in September 1937 he began to waiver. In Munich he saw a ceremonial parade of the SS, then he attended impressive army manoeuvres before visiting the great Krupp steel works and arms factories at Essen. In Berlin he and Hitler stood side by side to address a crowd of 800,000. A terrible cloudburst scattered the crowd and in the confusion that followed Mussolini, soaked and near to collapse due to exposure, was left to find his own way back to his accommodation. Despite this fiasco he was enormously impressed by the organisation and strength of the Nazi state which stood in such marked contrast to the apparent weakness and vacillation of Britain and France. In November the Duce told von Ribbentrop, a leading Nazi negotiator with foreign powers, that he was no longer interested in preserving Austria's independence.

On 5th November Hitler held a meeting with the heads of the armed forces and his Foreign Minister at the time, Baron von Neurath. Minutes of the meeting were kept by Hitler's adjutant, Colonel Hossbach. This document, known as the *Hossbach Memorandum*, fell into allied hands at the end of the Second World War and has provided material for the argument about whether Hitler was following a programme for the conquest of Europe or merely seizing chances presented to him by the inept leadership of Britain and France in order to fulfil age old German foreign policy objectives. The Führer gave an over-view of Germany's international situation as he saw it and proposed action to be taken in different circumstances. His main ideas are outlined by the quotes below:

- "The aim of German policy was to secure and preserve the racial community and to enlarge it. It was therefore a matter of space..."

- "Germany would always be faced by two hate-inspired antagonists, Britain and France."

- "Germany's problems could only be solved by means of force ..."

- "Germany had to act before 1943-1945 or the other powers would catch up in the arms race, just as Germany's weapons were becoming obsolete."

- "If France was weakened by civil war or involved in a war with a third power, probably Italy, the time had come for Germany to act."

- "For the improvement of our politico-military position our first objective, in the event of our being embroiled in war, must be to overthrow Czechoslovakia and Austria simultaneously in order to remove the threat to our flanks in any possible operation against the west."

- "Difficulties connected with the Empire, and the prospect of being once more entangled in a protracted European war, were decisive considerations for Britain against participation in a war with Germany... An attack by France without British support ... was hardly probable."

(*Documents in German Foreign Policy* Ser. D, Vol. I no.19.)

It should be noted that at this stage Hitler did not outline the exact course which he was to follow. When the time came he did not attack Czechoslovakia and Austria simultaneously. The Hossbach Memorandum does not suggest that the conquest of these countries should be followed by an attack on Poland. It does, however, give a number of useful insights into Hitler's strategic thinking. Commenting on this meeting, Professor Klaus Hildebrand, a leading member of the 'programme school' of German historians, wrote,

"...there was no longer any more talk of wanting to co-operate with and woo Britain - or rather blackmail and pressurise her - into an alliance. The tactics of barter and threat took a back seat. Hitler now adopted an 'ambivalent' course towards the British which acquired an increasingly anti-British flavour."
(from *The Foreign Policy of the Third Reich* by Klaus Hildebrand. Published by Batsford Books)

The Hossbach memorandum was used at the Nuremberg war crime trials after the Second World War, as evidence that the Nazis had sought war as a matter of policy. Historians who believe that Hitler planned for war accept the validity of this. In *Origins of the Second World War* AJP Taylor, the wayward genius of English historical writing, dismissed the Hossbach evidence. His claim is that the meeting was held to convince conservative military and financial experts, used by the Nazis, of the need to continue with the expensive rearmament programme and to isolate Schacht, the architect of Hitler's 'economic miracle', who opposed this. This may seem to beg the question, 'why was rearmament needed in the first place ?'

Elsewhere events soon moved in Hitler's direction. In January 1938 police raided the headquarters of the Austrian Nazi Party in the Teinfaltstrasse, Vienna. Later, Papen, now the German ambassador to Austria, sent home this memorandum:

"During the Teinfaltstrasse raid a memorandum written by Dr Tavs on the present situation fell into the hands of the police. Subject: the impossibility of progress under Schuschnigg, German invasion the only solution, thereafter formation of a government under Leopold."
(*Documents in German Foreign Policy* Ser. D Vol. 1 Doc. 279)

Captain Leopold and Dr Tavs were both Austrian Nazis. As a result, the Austrian Nazi Party was banned, in direct contravention of the secret part of the 1936 agreement. Hitler may have known nothing of the plot but the Austrian Chancellor, Kurt von Schuschnigg, decided that he should seek a meeting with the Führer. The two men met at Hitler's Bavarian mountain retreat, the Berghof at Berchtesgaden, on February 11th 1938.

Hitler immediately took the offensive, shouting down any attempt by Schuschnigg to defend himself from the accusation that he was persecuting patriotic Germans in Austria and building frontier defences against Germany. Two hours of screaming and shouting were followed by lunch at which Hitler switched to being a model of charm, but the Austrians noted the presence of a couple of German generals which seemed to underline the Führer's seriousness of purpose. After lunch, Hitler's terms were presented:

1 The ban on the Austrian Nazi party was to be lifted and the government was to recognise their loyalty to Austria.
2 Austrian Nazis were to hold the following key positions in government.
- Artur Seyss-Inquart was to be Minister of the Interior with control of the police.
- Glaise-Horstenau was to be Minister for War. The German and Austrian armies were to have officer exchanges.
- Fischbok was to be Minister for Finance and the economic systems of the two countries were to be assimilated.
3 Imprisoned Nazis were to be released and officers and officials who had been sacked because of their Nazi connections were to be reinstated.

These terms were designed to turn Austria into Hitler's puppet state. Schuschnigg eventually left, having agreed, with great reluctance, to implement the agreement within three days.

When appointed to office the new Nazi ministers acted with complete disregard for the Chancellor and the amnestied Nazis, who re-emerged into public life, caused disturbances all over Austria. Against the advice of Mussolini, Schuschnigg decided to hold a plebiscite on March 13th to ask the Austrians if they wanted an Austria which was "free, independent, Christian and German". Hitler was furious and ordered his army to prepare to invade Austria. To Mussolini he sent an explanation of his actions (he was acting on behalf of the Germans in Austria who were oppressed by their own government) and a promise that he accepted the Brenner Pass as the permanent frontier between Germany and Italy. *[See Source 15]* That day, 11th March, Italy's Foreign Minister wrote in his diary,

"The French Chargé d'Affaires asked to come and see me ... in order to form a concerted plan for the Austrian situation. I replied that we had no intention of consulting with anybody ... After sanctions and non-recognition of the Empire and all the other miseries inflicted on us since 1935, do they expect to rebuild Stresa in an hour, with Hannibal at the gates? Thanks to their policy France and England have lost Austria. For us too it is not an advantage. But in the meantime we have acquired Abyssinia."
(*Ciano's Diary. 1937-38* Translated by A Mayor page 87)

On March 11th the Czech government was promised that "Czechoslovakia has nothing to fear from the Reich" and in return they promised not to mobilise their army. That same day Seyss-Inquart and Glaise-Horstenau presented Hitler's demand for the cancellation of the plebiscite. When this was finally conceded, the resignation of Schuschnigg and his replacement by Seyss-Inquart was added. Seyss-Inquart had instructions that he was to telegram for help from the German army as soon as he was in office. Eventually, and with great reluctance, old President Miklas of Austria acceded to these demands. Seyss-Inquart requested that German troops should not invade Austria, but despite this German troops crossed the border at dawn on Saturday 12th March. It was not the most impressive invasion in military history, as seventy percent of German armoured vehicles broke down, but this did not affect the outcome.

Hitler spent the following night in his home town of Linz, which he had left as a penniless, petulant nobody in 1907. He was greeted with such enthusiasm that he decided not to set up a puppet government, but to establish direct rule, with Austria as a mere province of the Reich. Ciano recognised the popularity of the Anschluss in Austria,

"*March 14th.* ....Berger too maintains that Italy could not have acted differently - if a single Italian soldier had entered Austria, the whole population of the country, with the exception of the Jews, would have fired on us."
(*Ciano's Diary* Translated by A Mayor p89.)

On March 13th Hitler entered Vienna in triumph. Himmler was already there to supervise the SS and the Gestapo who were rounding up the opposition. When a plebiscite was eventually held, 99.75% of Austrians voted for the new arrangements. The Nazis knew how to fix these things. Naturally the British government protested, in the strongest terms. *[See Source 17]* Charlie Chaplin was probably more effective. He made a hilarious film about the incident which features a magnificent character analysis of two dictators, Adenoid Hynkel of Tomania and Benzino Napoloni of Bacteria, as they debate the fate of Osterich. The film is called *The Great Dictator*. It was not shown in Germany.

The Anschluss had proved to Hitler, yet again, that he could get away with international bullying. He would use these tactics again. It also gave him control of Austria's useful iron and steel industries and provided a springboard for the invasion of southeastern Europe should he ever feel so inclined. His attention now turned to Czechoslovakia whose strategically important western provinces were now virtually surrounded by Germany. (See map p39)

7   THE CZECH CRISIS

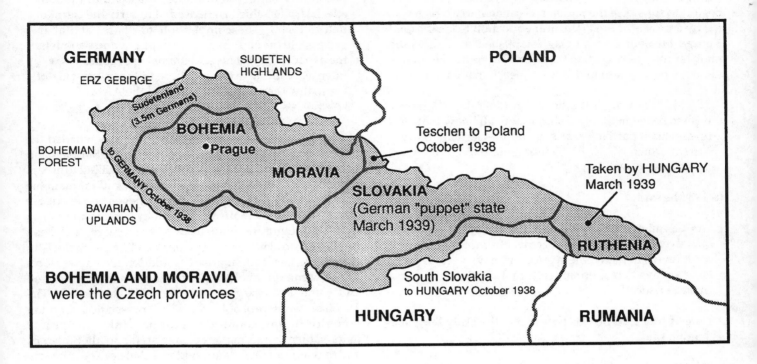

After the Anschluss Hitler's attention soon turned to Czechoslovakia, the other state which his aide, Colonel Hossbach, said the Führer had decided to attack when the opportunity presented itself.

He had many reasons to dislike Czechoslovakia. In his view it was peopled by Slavonic 'Untermenschen', whose long-standing opposition to German rule in the old Austrian Empire, especially their 'treachery' during the First World War when they deserted in droves to fight for the Russians, had helped to destroy it. Czechoslovakia was the only really successful democratic state created by the hated Versailles settlement, and it was an amalgam of different peoples. There were Czechs in the western provinces of Bohemia and Moravia, Slovaks in the central province of Slovakia and Ruthenes in the east in Ruthenia. There were also a number of minority nationals scattered about, such as Hungarian Magyars, and more significantly three million Germans, former subjects of Austria, living in the western fringe of the country which was known as the Sudetenland. While the other states created at Versailles lapsed into dictatorship, chaos, or both, Czechoslovakia proved that ethnically different people can live together in democratic peace, an idea which was anathema to the Nazis. The Czechs were ardent supporters of the League of Nations, a body whose principles were totally at odds with Nazi dogma since it defended the rights of small nations against the aggression of larger ones. They were also allied to France and Russia, Germany's sworn enemies. (Hitler's dislike of Czechoslovakia was no doubt inflamed by the Czech 'Untermenschen' defeating the 11 chosen representatives of his 'master race' 3 - 1 in the semi-finals of the 1934 World Cup. Hitler was not a good sport and no doubt took some small pleasure in avenging this defeat, off the park)

When Czechoslovakia had been created, the western district, the Sudetenland, with its German population, had been included because it gave the new state a strong natural frontier in the form of an encircling mountain chain (the Bohemian forest, the Erz Gebirge and the Sudeten Highlands). On grounds of self-determination, rather than 'real-politik', this area would have gone to Germany. The Czechs spent a lot of time and money improving on nature and created a formidable defensive barrier between themselves and Germany. Their army was known to be well organised and efficient and backed by an indigenous arms industry which included the famous Skoda works. Hitler knew that he could not move against either Poland or Russia so long as Czechoslovakia remained free, projecting out into Germany like a thorn in her side. The airfields of the Sudetenland could be used as bases for French or Russian aircraft to launch bomber raids on any of the important German cities or their troops could come down from the mountains and invade the Fatherland.

Although the Czechs could not be accused of neglecting their own defences, they did have their worries. Many doubted the strength and also reliability of France as an ally and her ability to help in the defence of a country separated from her by the bulk of Germany. Russia might well be reluctant to take on Germany on her own and, even if she decided to aid the Czechs, her forces would not get leave to pass through ,or overfly, Poland or Rumania, both of which were anti-Russian because of ancient enmities.

While the Generals of the Wehrmacht were acutely aware of both the number of divisions available to Czechoslovakia's allies and the strength of her own defences, Hitler was sensitive to the political divisions and lack of will to resist in France and to Czechoslovakia's consequent isolation.

The Sudeten Germans were the only national group who had completely failed to fit into the new Czechoslovakia. As the former Imperial ruling nation they resented their loss of status. Even before Hitler took power in Germany Nazi ideas and organisation began to take root among them. During 1935 the German Foreign Office secretly began to subsidise the Sudeten German Party which was led by a power hungry physical education teacher called Konrad Henlein who quickly established himself as the main spokesman of the Sudeten Germans. Henlein's ideology can be gathered from a speech made in 1931.

"We declare war to the death on Liberalism ... men wish to be led in manly fashion ... We all know that an un-German parliamentarism, an un-German party system which divides into inorganic parts, will and must break down."

In 1936 he said,

"As Germans in the Sudeten provinces ... we feel ourselves as members of the great cultural community of Germans in the whole world, and have here, as we have always had, German cultural tasks to carry out characteristically."

As late as July 1938 he was reported in the *Daily Telegraph* as having said,

"Nothing short of full autonomy will be acceptable to us ... We do not ask to be annexed to the German Reich."
(quoted in *Britain and Germany between the Wars* by Martin Gilbert pp. 107 - 110)

Henlein's party won 62% of the Sudeten German vote in elections in 1935. In 1937 the Czech government, well aware of the danger they faced, made strenuous efforts to come to terms with the Sudetens. Hitler displayed great cunning at this stage. He entered the arena as the champion of an oppressed minority, presenting the issue as one of a fair deal for the Sudetens and not as a demand for the transfer of the territory to Germany. Henlein had visited Berlin in March 1938. He told a German official of his conversation with the Führer. The details were recorded.

"The Führer stated that he intended to settle the Sudeten German question in the not too distant future ... He told Henlein that he (Henlein) was the rightful leader of the Sudeten German element ... To Henlein's objection that he, Henlein, could only be a substitute Hitler replied : I will stand for you; from tomorrow you will be my Viceroy."
(*Documents in German Foreign Policy* Ser. D Vol. 2 Doc 107)

Henlein was told to make demands which the Czechs could not meet. He later said that Hitler's orders were that "we must always demand so much that we can never be satisfied". Hitler intended to cause so much trouble in the Sudetenland that he could intervene on the pretext of protecting the Germans and preventing a civil war. The Anschluss with Austria had already engendered wild excitement with huge Nazi parades through the streets of major towns as the Sudetens anticipated liberation by Hitler.

In May Hitler took steps to square his plans for Czechoslovakia with Mussolini. Professor Alan Bullock describes the situation vividly.

"The invitation had been given when Mussolini was in Germany the autumn before. Every party boss and Nazi Party hanger-on tried to squeeze into the four special trains which were needed to carry the German delegation ... The competition to share, at Italian expense, in the endless galas, receptions and banquets, the expensive presents and imposing decorations was intense. Nothing appealed more to the gutter-elite of Germany than a free trip south of the Alps."
(Alan Bullock *Hitler a Study in Tyranny* p.444)

Hitler's championship of German minorities worried the Italians since they had their own version of the Sudetenland in the South Tyrol but Mussolini seemed willing to accept Hitler's guarantees that the alpine crest would remain the frontier and that these 'Volk' would never be part of the 'Reich'. After Italy took over the South Tyrol from Austria in 1919 a vigorous 'Italianisation' campaign had been implemented. The region's name was changed to the Alto Adige, the German language forbidden in schools, local self-government abolished, private property confiscated and some Tyrolese forced to adopt Italian names. The Tyrolese were probably the most persecuted German minority in any country in Europe. Hitler completely ignored them, while making a huge fuss about the Sudetens and the Germans in Poland, evidence that he used minority problems to manufacture arguments with the states he chose to attack. (Today the boot is on the other foot in the South Tyrol. The region is still part of Italy, but the Italians there complain that they are terrorised by the Tyrolese.)

Meanwhile, Britain and France, anxious to avoid trouble, had been urging the Czechs to placate Henlein and reach an agreement with the Sudetens. Lord Halifax, the British Foreign Secretary, informed the delighted Germans, through his ambassador in Berlin , of the British action.

Hitler had already told his Generals to draw up a plan, code name 'Operation Green', to smash Czechoslovakia by military action after a period of contrived and orchestrated diplomatic crises. [*See Souce 18*] On May 20th, in response to rumoured German troop movements, the Czech army was ordered to mobilise. This was exactly what Hitler wanted. He could now accuse the Czechs of being provocative and of threatening Germany. He would be forced to "act in self- defence". To his surprise and fury he received a warning from Britain and France of the dangers of war if Czechoslovakia were to be attacked and both France and Russia reaffirmed their obligation to help his intended prey. Hitler had expected no such unity among the European powers. The outcome of what came to be known as 'the May Crisis' was that he was forced to eat humble pie, protesting that he had no aggressive intent towards the Czechs. After this humiliation he was more determined than ever to mutilate Czechoslovakia and laid his plans while quietly fuming at his Berghof.

The Western powers probably drew the wrong conclusions from this incident. Instead of noting the effect of standing up to Hitler, they blamed President Benes of Czechoslovakia for precipitating a quite unnecessary crisis. In the summer of 1938 things moved Hitler's way again. General Keitel was told that 'Operation Green' would be implemented by 1st October at the latest. Hitler knew that Britain and France were putting pressure on the Czechs to make concessions to the Sudetens and that Benes must have felt very isolated as a result. Sir Neville Henderson, Britain's Ambassador to Berlin, wrote in July 1938,

"I honestly believe that the moment has come for Prague to get a real twist of the screw ... It is the French job, but if they won't face it I believe we will have to do it. "

and later,

"...I fear that the Czechs as a whole are an incorrigibly pig-headed people."
(*Documents in British Foreign Policy* as quoted by Martin Gilbert)

Hitler worked on that isolation. Rumania was urged not to let Russian forces cross her territory. Diplomatic sources reported that Poland remained anti-Russian and the Poles were encouraged in their demands for Teschen, part of Silesia that had gone to Czechoslovakia instead of to Poland in 1919. The Hungarians were urged to keep up their demands for Slovakia , part of which was inhabited by Magyars, the people of Hungary. The Hungarians, however, while keen to get the land, were wary of Germany and reluctant to project themselves into a quarrel with Czechoslovakia's nominal allies in the 'little entente', Yugoslavia and Rumania. Their caution infuriated Hitler but Polish and Hungarian demands nevertheless made the situation more difficult for the Czechs.

Despite the gathering storm the British and French made no effort to involve Russia, a country which had signed pacts with both France and Czechoslovakia in 1935. This was mainly due to a distaste for 'Bolshevism' in the largely Conservative National Government of Neville Chamberlain. Hitler was seen as a lesser threat than Stalin. The Russians also suspected that the western democracies would like to stand back and watch them slug it out with the Germans in a war which would weaken both their main enemies.

Henlein made numerous visits to Germany at this time. He continued to negotiate with the Benes government, always taking care not to reach an agreement, even when the Sudetens were offered 'home rule'. He kept the German minority in a constant state of agitation and provoked numerous incidents between Czech officials and local Sudetens.

The senior officers of the German army were, almost to a man, convinced that Hitler was leading Germany along a very dangerous path which would lead to an unwinnable rerun of the Great War, fighting Britain, France and Russia on two fronts with an inadequately prepared army. A fierce argument with Hitler led to the resignation of the Chief of Staff, General Ludwig Beck. Beck soon became involved in a conspiracy to arrest Hitler and put him on trial before a people's court because he had endangered Germany by his rashness. Beck is also said to have developed a revulsion for Nazi human rights abuses. This plot simmered on for years but the conspirators never managed to organise themselves sufficiently to achieve anything until the bomb plot of 20th July 1944 when Colonel Klaus von Stauffenberg left a briefcase full of explosives under the table in Hitler's headquarters. The

resulting explosion, very close to the Führer, killed several people and blew off one of Hitler's trouser legs. In the aftermath Stauffenberg and several others were shot, eight senior officers were slowly hanged with piano wires from meat hooks, while Beck and the great Rommel were allowed to commit suicide. For Beck it was the end of a long road which had begun six years earlier with the Czech crisis.

The success which Czechoslovakia had enjoyed between 1929 and 1938 was largely due to two men: Thomas Masaryk, her first President, and his Foreign Minister, Eduard Benes, who followed him as President on his resignation and death in 1935. Benes was a sure-footed democrat and negotiator with a fine instinct for compromise. He decided that Henlein's game had to be brought to an end. The Sudeten leader was asked to a meeting at the Presidential Palace and offered a blank cheque. Benes was willing to agree to all eight demands which Henlein had made in his keynote policy speech at Karlsbad in April of that year, even home rule for the Sudetens. [*See Source 19*] He was invited to write his demand on a piece of blank paper. It seemed as if jelly had finally been nailed to the wall and Henlein no longer had any room to manoeuvre. However he used the current disturbances as an excuse not to talk. Only when "brutal Czech officials" who had beaten up "innocent Germans" had been punished could negotiations begin. Benes had proved beyond all doubt that Sudeten grievances were not the real point at issue. Henlein left for Germany in a hurry.

In the meantime leaders of the conspiracy against Hitler were in London seeking evidence that the British and French would help the Czechs. They intended to use this to persuade others to join them but they got little of substance other than a letter from Winston Churchill, whom some regarded, at that time, as the mad dog of British politics, always growling for rearmament and looking for somebody to bite. The ground was cut from below their feet by *The Times*, seen by many foreigners as the mouthpiece of the British establishment, which advocated, in an editorial, that Czechoslovakia should be obliged to cede the Sudetenland to Germany.

In a speech at a party rally in Nuremberg on 12th September Hitler launched a violent attack on Benes. He compared the Sudetens to the Palestinian Arabs whose homeland was being taken over by the Jews, but promised that the Sudetens would not go undefended. This had an immediate effect in the Sudetenland where riots broke out in the main towns. The Czechs did not panic. Martial law was proclaimed, a few rioters were shot and by the middle of the month the situation was under control and Henlein had taken refuge in Bavaria. The Nazi press made as much as they could of the situation they had created, accusing the Czechs of inflicting "a reign of terror" on the Sudetens, but the fact remained that they had failed to cause Czechoslovakia to disintegrate under the pressure. It seemed that Hitler would either have to stand down or resort to direct aggression and send his army against the Czech defences.

At this stage Britain and France broke under the strain in a way which the Czechs had not. Eduard Daladier, the French Prime Minister, urged Chamberlain to initiate negotiations and get the best deal he could from Hitler.

Chamberlain, a believer in face to face negotiations, sent a message to Hitler offering to fly to Germany to meet him. Hitler was delighted. The mountain would come to Mohammed! The British Prime Minister, a man of 69 who had never flown before, would cross Europe to beg for peace. This would go a long way towards expunging the shame of 1918. A meeting was fixed for 15th September at the Berghof. Chamberlain's action of flying to Germany was subsequently regarded by many as a mistake and seen as a sign of weakness. This is perhaps unfair to Chamberlain. It must have taken considerable moral strength to put aside feelings of personal pride and status and fly to Germany in an uncomfortable, noisy aeroplane in the hope of averting war. It was the act of a statesman, even if a misguided one, and it showed a type of strength which Nazis did not even begin to comprehend.

A gruelling seven hour flight on 15th September led to a meeting at 4 pm. Hitler was at pains to point out how good he had been as Chancellor, signing the Anglo-German Naval Pact, renouncing Germany's claim to Alsace-Lorraine and making a non-aggression pact with Poland. He could not afford to be so generous with the Sudetenland since it involved the question of race and a persecuted German population which had to be brought into the Reich . All suggestions that this was purely a question of protecting minority rights were now dropped. Hitler made it clear that the Polish and Hungarian claims also had to be met. He stressed that,

> "The return to the Reich of the 3 million Germans in Czechoslovakia he (the Führer) would make possible at all costs. He would face any war, and even the risk of a world war, for this..."
> "The Czechoslovak question would then, of course, be the last major problem to be solved..."
> "Finally, Germany would, of course, always continue to press her demand for colonies; this was at any rate not a warlike demand. However, it would have to be granted one day..."
> (German minutes of the meeting from *Documents in German Foreign Policy* Ser. D Vol 2 Doc 562)

Hitler brushed aside all attempts by Chamberlain to discuss the practical considerations of how the transfer might be made without creating fresh minority rights problems. Chamberlain was annoyed and accused Hitler of wasting his time by allowing him to come to Germany when he had no intention of negotiating and meant to use force. Faced with a more determined adversary Hitler softened his attitude and conceded that, if the British government would openly agree in principle to the ceding of the Sudetenland to Germany, talks could go on. Chamberlain, urging Hitler to do nothing rash in the meantime, returned to Britain to put this proposal to the British cabinet as a prelude to a second meeting. *[See Source 20]*

Hitler thought that it would be impossible to get the Czechs to agree to hand over the Sudetenland. He had secured Chamberlain's agreement to this on grounds of self-determination. If the British cabinet agreed but Czechoslovakia refused, Britain would blame her and not Hitler for the subsequent war. Hitler began to orchestrate the chorus of opposition to Czechoslovakia. He authorised the formation of a Sudeten Freikorps, which promptly seized control of the Sudeten towns, and increased the German military presence along the border. He prompted the Poles and Hungarians to reaffirm their territorial demands. The Slovak Peoples Party, which probably did not represent the wishes of the majority of the Slovaks, was induced to ask for home rule from the Czechs.

Despite Hitler's hopes to the contrary, Chamberlain was able to get the consent of both his cabinet and the French government to the plan. The reluctant Czechs were bullied into accepting it.

On 22nd September 1938, Chamberlain flew to Bad Godesberg on the Rhine where he was to meet Hitler. He was confident of success because his proposals appeared to meet all the German demands. Not only was Germany to get the Sudetenland without any plebiscite, but also the alliances between Czechoslovakia and France and Russia were to be replaced by an international guarantee of Czech independence. What he failed to see was that this scheme would deny Hitler the pleasure of smashing Czechoslovakia, while flouting international opposition, and that this was what he wanted above all else.

When the two men met, Hitler immediately said that the situation had changed. He was unable to offer a very convincing account of how it had changed but he did mention the demands of the Poles and the Hungarians and worked himself into a fury over the indignities he claimed the Sudetens had suffered. He demanded the immediate withdrawal of the Czech army from the Sudetenland so that the Germans could take over by 1st October.

These new demands did not call for very much more than was already on offer. They were clearly the work of a man looking for a fight. This puzzled, hurt and annoyed Chamberlain. It was behaviour so alien to him that he could not even begin to understand it. He protested, angrily, that he had, in good faith, staked his whole career and reputation on securing the package he had offered Hitler and now he found it rejected for no good reason .

At this point news arrived that the Czech army had mobilised. Hitler demanded the complete evacuation of the Sudetenland by 28th September but then, with a great show of magnanimity he softened and, as "a final concession", reverted to 1st October as the date for Czech withdrawal.

Chamberlain said that he would submit these new demands to the British, French and Czech governments. Despite the shameful way in which he had been treated, he felt that he and Hitler had developed a feeling of mutual confidence in the two days of the meeting. It is the prerequisite of a successful confidence trick that the victim wants to believe that he is getting a good deal. Chamberlain went to Godesberg believing that he could and would come to terms with Hitler. Strangely, he continued to believe this afterwards. *[See Source 21]*

On his return to Britain, the Prime Minister presented the dictator's demands to his cabinet, who proved unwilling either to accept them or to attempt to force them on the Czechs. The following day Hitler addressed a Nazi rally in

The entry of German troops into Sudetenland

the Berlin Sportspalast. *[See Source 22]* He already knew the decision of the British Cabinet. His speech was a violent attack on Czechoslovakia and its Prime Minister, Benes, who was accused of organising a campaign of persecution and terror against all the non-Czech peoples of his country, Slovaks, Magyars, Poles and especially Germans. The brutality of this campaign, Hitler claimed, had resulted in a flow of refugees which had risen to over 200,000 a day. (If this had been true it would have cleared the Sudetenland of its German population in about a fortnight!) Benes felt safe to do this, Hitler said, because of the support of Britain, France and Russia. He was encouraging the Russians to use Czech airfields as bases from which to bomb Germany. This vile assault on an innocent people had led to the Führer's demand at the Berchtesgaden Berghof for the ceding of the Sudetenland to Germany. Faced with the might of Germany and denied the support of his allies, Benes had been forced to agree. At Godesberg, Hitler said, he had merely demanded that Benes keep his promise and do so quickly. Unless Germany got satisfaction

there would be war. This situation had been forced on the Germans and Benes would have to decide - war or peace.. Significantly, Hitler then said that the world should know that Germany had changed. It was no longer the Germany of 1918 but was united and determined. His determination to atone for the shame of defeat in the First World War had emerged yet again as a major factor in his motivation. He made it clear that he intended to take the Sudetenland even if it meant war with Britain and France.

The Führer's confidence and enthusiasm was far from universal in Germany . The army high command warned him that he would have to commit most of the Wehrmacht to the assault on the Czech defences, leaving the Rhine forces outnumbered five to one by the French. Once again the army plotters were at work but in the end they neither arrested nor assassinated Hitler. When armoured vehicles were paraded through the streets of the German capital, they were greeted, not by cheers and enthusiasm, but by a silent people who turned away in distress. If Germany was not the Germany of 1918, it wasn't the Germany of 1914 either and this lack of popular enthusiasm would not have escaped Hitler's notice. Then came the news that Britain's Royal Navy had been mobilised for war. On 'Black Wednesday' (28th September 1938) trenches were being dug in London and the entrances to important buildings sandbagged. In capitals throughout Europe an atmosphere of gloom and despondency prevailed. War seemed unavoidable. Just then Hitler backed off very slightly. In a communiqué to Chamberlain, justifying his stance, he half suggested that it might be worth Chamberlain's time to continue with his peace initiative.

At this point the French put forward another plan to give Germany the Sudetenland in stages, starting on 1st October. Ciano recorded,

> "Septmeber 28. 10am Four hours to go before the outbreak of hostilities, when Perth (British Ambassador in Rome) telephones to ask for an interview. I receive him at once. He says, with much emotion, that Chamberlain appeals to the Duce for his friendly intervention in these hours, which he considers the last in which something can be done to save peace and civilisation. He repeats the guarantee offered by England and France for the return of the Sudetenland. I ask Perth whether I am to regard his démarche as an official invitation to the Duce to assume the role of mediator. Yes ... I go to the Duce ... He telephones Attolico: 'Go to the Führer and tell him, having first said that in any eventuality I shall be at his side, that I recommend that the commencement of hostilities should be delayed for 24 hours. Meanwhile I undertake to study what can be done to solve the problem.'"
>
> (Ciano's Diary 1937-1938 Translated by A Mayor p 165)

After his adventures in Abyssinia and Spain, Mussolini was not yet ready for another war. He consulted with Hitler who agreed to the conference on condition that the Duce himself would attend. Mussolini was offered Frankfurt or Munich as the choice of venues. He chose Munich. The British and French Prime Ministers, Chamberlain and Daladier, were to represent their countries but the Czechs and Russians were not to be invited. Once again Chamberlain had to take to the air in a hurry. It was at this point that he made the often quoted remark,

> "How horrible, fantastic, incredible it is that we should be digging trenches and trying on gas masks here because of a quarrel in a far away country between people of whom we know nothing. War is a fearful thing and we must be very clear before we embark on it that it is the really great issues that are at stake."

The conference began shortly after noon the next day.

THE MUNICH CONFERENCE

When the delegations assembled, on 29th September 1938, Mussolini was at an advantage as he could speak the languages of the other delegates. He assumed a leading role. [See Source 23] Hitler once again refused to agree to Czech or Russian participation. The conference lacked any formal organisation. There were no minutes kept, no agenda, no Chairperson but after much haggling and

bargaining an agreement was reached. Hitler got more or less what he had demanded at Godesberg. The Sudetenland was to be his on 1st October and then plebiscites, supervised by an International Commission representing Britain, France, Italy, Germany and Czechoslovakia, but not Russia, would be held to decide the future of marginal areas with substantial German populations. Hitler had emphasised that this was his last territorial claim in Europe and that he did not want to pollute the Reich by the inclusion of non-Germans. Britain and France guaranteed the rest of Czechoslovakia against aggression. Germany and Italy promised to join them once Poland and Hungary had been satisfied. The task of informing the Czechs of the details of the deal was left to their allies, the British and French. Chamberlain flew back to Britain. Waving the agreement which bore Hitler's signature, he said on his arrival at Heston Airport,

> "My good friends, this is the second time in our history that there has come back from Germany to Downing Street peace with honour. I believe it is peace for our time."

As Chamberlain was driven from the airfield to Buckingham Palace to report to the King cheering people lined his route. In Downing Street the crowds sang 'For he's a jolly good fellow'.

Not everybody agreed. Winston Churchill, for years a voice crying in the political wilderness, advocating rearmament and denouncing appeasement, said,

> "He had to choose between war and dishonour. He has chosen dishonour. He will get war." [See Source 25]

Chamberlain defended his achievement in the Commons during a debate on Munich on October 3rd,

> "The path which leads to appeasement is long and bristles with obstacles. The question of Czechoslovakia is the latest and perhaps most dangerous. Now that we have got past it, I feel that it may be possible to make further progress along the road to sanity." (Hansard)

Clement Attlee (Labour) said,

> "We have been unable to go in for carefree rejoicing. We have felt we are in the midst of tragedy. We have felt humiliation. This is not a victory for reason and humanity. It has been a victory for brute force... We have seen today a gallant, civilised and democratic people betrayed and handed over to a ruthless despotism." (Hansard)

On 1st October 1938 German troops entered the Sudetenland. Poland took Teschen and Hungary seized South Slovakia with its large Magyar population. Shortly afterwards Benes resigned and the neo-fascist government which took office promised to co-operate with the Germans. Communism was banned and anti-Jewish measures initiated.

The German Generals who examined Czechoslovakia's frontier defences were distinctly relieved that it had not been necessary to take them by force. In March 1939, when

Hitler broke another of his promises and took the rest of the Czech lands, they gratefully received, intact and undamaged, the great Skoda arms factory and the Brno small arms works, not to mention 2,200 artillery pieces, 600 tanks and 750 aircraft. Germany's military strength had been enhanced.

The Czech affair served to increase Hitler's prestige in Germany. He himself gained in confidence since he had read the situation correctly and his generals had been proved wrong. With the Czech threat removed from his southeastern flank he was now free to take action on Germany's eastern frontier against Poland or Russia. Britain and France had lost the possible services of a strong ally in Czechoslovakia. Despite all this, Hitler seems to have been annoyed at Chamberlain for denying him the pleasure of defying the democracies and ripping Czechoslovakia apart by military force.

Britain had secured a few more months to rearm and build up her air force while observing whether Hitler was, or was not, a man of his word.

The Russians were deeply offended and their suspicions of Britain and France were reinforced. They had been willing to act to help control Hitler and hadn't even been invited to Munich. On their own there was little they could do since their troops could not cross hostile Poland and Rumania. Potential opposition to Hitler in the future had been badly divided.

Historians will argue endlessly over whether Britain and France should have fought to defend Czechoslovakia, but it didn't take Hitler long to prove just how empty his promises were. No plebiscites were ever held to determine the new border and in March 1939 German troops dismembered the rest of Czechoslovakia. Slovakia became a nominally independent German puppet state while the Czech provinces of Bohemia and Moravia became a German protectorate. Up to this point Hitler had justified his demands and actions in terms of self-determination. This was impossible with his actions in March 1939. Appeasement was dead.

Hitler, of course, was not short of an explanation for his actions:

> "Germany a few months ago was compelled, in the face of the intolerable terrorist regime of Czechoslovakia, to take under its protection German

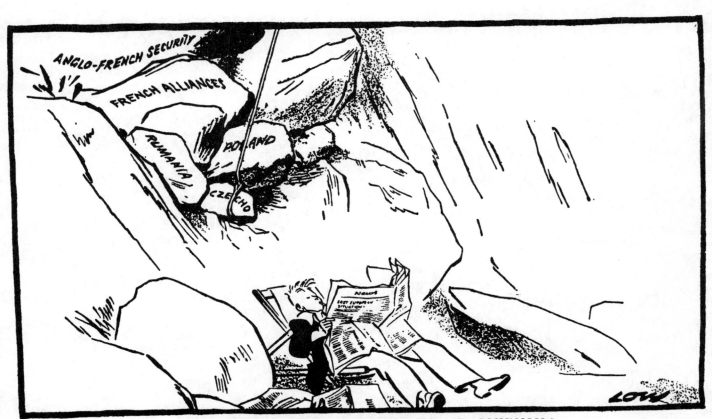

WHAT'S CZECHOSLOVAKIA TO ME, ANYWAY ?

45

fellow-countrymen living in self-contained areas of settlement; during the last few weeks similar features have reappeared with increasing frequency ... numerous Germans have once more fallen victim to this violence. Every hour the appeals for help from the sufferers and persecuted become more frequent. From the populous islands of German speech which the magnanimity of Germany last autumn allowed to remain as part of Czechoslovakia there begins to flow once more into the Reich a stream of fugitives who have been driven from house and home. ...to put a stop to this threat to peace...I have determined to allow German troops to march into Bohemia and Moravia."

(*The Speeches of Adolf Hitler* edited by N Baynes page 1585)

Postcript

In the grounds of the British Aluminium Company's Fort William factory stands the case of a huge bomb dropped by Germany's Luftwaffe during the Second World War. Local tradition has it that its failure to explode was due to deliberate sabotage by the Czechs who assembled it in the Skoda works. Hitler's gains in March '39 may not be so easy to evaluate !

In the graveyard of the old Chapel of St. Duthac in Tain, Scotland, lie the remains of a Czech aircrew who were based at RAF Tain during the Second World War. It seems that their Liberator was badly shot up over Norway, but they managed to limp home to base only to crash on the adjacent golf course. What was it like on that last terrible flight ? One can imagine a wounded pilot, weak with loss of blood, struggling with the controls of a damaged aircraft, a surge of hope when the Ross-shire coastline was sighted and then the catastrophic loss of control. In the ninety minutes or so that it would have taken them to fly back from Norway to their deaths did those Czech airmen, so far from home, ponder the wisdom and justice of Munich?

AGREEMENT REACHED ON SEPTEMBER 29, 1938, BETWEEN GERMANY, THE UNITED KINGDOM, FRANCE AND ITALY AT MUNICH

Germany, the United Kingdom, France, and Italy, taking into consideration the agreement, which has been already reached in principle for the cession to Germany of the Sudeten German territory, have agreed on the following terms and conditions governing the said cession and the measures consequent thereon, and by this agreement they each hold themselves responsible for the steps necessary to secure its fulfilment.

1)   The evacuation will begin on October 1st.

2)   The United Kingdom, France, and Italy agree that the evacuation of the territory shall be completed by October 10th, without any existing installations having been destroyed, and that the Czechoslovak Government will be held responsible for carrying out the evacuation without damage to the said installations.

3)   The conditions governing the evacuation will be laid down in detail by an international commission composed of representatives of Germany, the United Kingdom, France, Italy and Czechoslovakia.

Neville Chamberlain with the document "Peace in Our Time" at Heston.

4) The occupation by stages of the predominantly German territories marked on the attached map will be occupied by German troops in the following order: the territory marked number I on the 1st and 2nd of October, the territory marked number II on the 2nd and 3rd of October, the territory marked number III on the 3rd, 4th and 5th of October, the territory marked number IV on the 6th and 7th of October. The remaining territory of preponderantly German character will be ascertained by the aforesaid international commission forthwith and be occupied by German troops by the 19th of October.

5) The international commission referred to in paragraph 3) will determine the territories in which a plebiscite is to be held. These territories will be occupied by international bodies until the plebiscite has been completed. The same commission will fix the conditions in which the plebiscite is to be held, taking as a basis the conditions of the Saar plebiscite. The commission will also fix a date, not later than the end of November, on which the plebiscite will beheld.

6) The final determination of the frontiers will be carried out by the international commission. This commission will also be entitled to recommend to the four Powers, Germany, the United Kingdom, France and Italy, in certain exceptional cases, minor modifications in the strictly ethnographical determination of the zones which are to be transferred without plebiscite.

7) There will be a right of option into and out of the transferred territories, the option to be exercised within 6 months from the date of this agreement. A German-Czechoslovak commission shall determine the details of the option, consider ways of facilitating the transfer of population and settle questions of principle arising out of the said transfer.

8) The Czechoslovak Government will, within a period of 4 weeks from the date of this agreement, release from their military and police forces any Sudeten Germans who may wish to be released, and the Czechoslovak Government will within the same period release Sudeten German prisoners who are serving terms of imprisonment for political offences.

ADOLF HITLER   ED. DALADIER
MUSSOLINI   NEVILLE CHAMBERLAIN

From *Documents in Foreign Policy*. Series D. Vol. II. Doc. 675 (H.M.S.O.)

8 POLAND AND THE OUTBREAK OF WAR

The destruction of Czechoslovakia made it obvious, even to those who were desperate to be deceived, that Hitler's promises and guarantees were completely worthless. He was neither a man of honour nor a man of his word and had told the same lie, "I have no other territorial claims after this", far too often for anybody to believe it any more. The leaders of Britain and France were forced to accept the need to plan for an imminent war with Germany.

Ultimately Hitler could be expected to attack France, but Poland and the Polish corridor seemed a much more likely target for his next offensive. The countries of southeast Europe, the Balkans, were also a possibility, but Germany had established such economic and political domination there that this seemed a less likely area for Nazi expansion.

For centuries the Poles had regarded themselves as a nation. In 1772, however, their country had been partitioned between Prussia, the dominant kingdom of north Germany, the Holy Roman Empire, which was neither Holy nor Roman but in fact Austrian, and the Russia of Catherine II. In 1815, after the defeat of Napoleon who had reunited the Poles, the great powers considered the fate of Poland. They rejected its unification and independence, not so much on the grounds of their alleged hostility to nationalism, but because they felt that Poland had no chance of survival , surrounded as she was by strong predatory states. In 1919 the great powers, following Woodrow Wilson's doctrine of self-determination, resurrected the Polish Nation. The boundaries were very hard to define. Prussian expansion eastwards had created many areas of mixed population and there was a lack of convenient natural frontiers such as mountains or big rivers. East Prussia was separated from the rest of Germany by the ceding of West Prussia to Poland to enable her to have access to the sea. This strip of land became known as the 'Polish Corridor'. It contained the city of Danzig (Gdansk to the Poles) which became a 'free city' run by the League of Nations so that both Germany and Poland could use it as a sea port. Farther south, in Silesia, Poland received territory which had originally been German and where German capital had developed mining and industry which had attracted so many Polish workers that Poles had become the majority there.

The Polish settlement was probably the aspect of the Versailles Treaty which was most resented in Germany and the one which the most Germans wanted revised. There were many reasons for hostility between the Catholic Poles and the Protestant Prussians, but Hitler, who came from Catholic Austria, did not share these feelings. In 1934 he had actually signed a non-aggression pact with Poland.

At the end of 1938 the German Foreign Ministry proposed to Poland that Danzig should be returned to Germany, although Poland's use of it would be guaranteed, and that Poland should allow a German controlled road and railway to be built across the corridor to East Prussia. It was suggested that Poland might like to become Germany's ally against Russia. These demands were seen as the thin end of a wedge by Poland's Foreign Minister, Colonel Beck, and he refused to accede to them. The only country big enough and close enough to offer Poland practical assistance in the face of German aggression was another of her ancient oppressors, Russia. Belatedly Beck began to build diplomatic bridges.

German Seizure of Memel

In March 1939, after the destruction of Czechoslovakia, Hitler turned on Lithuania, a small Baltic state made independent from Russia in 1919. He demanded the return of Memel, a city and strip of land bordering East Prussia, which naturally had a substantial German population. Lithuania was in no position to resist this demand and Poland saw how Hitler intended to conduct international relations in the Baltic. In late March Hitler renewed his demands on Poland. At this stage he seemed willing to permit her continued existence if she would hand over Danzig and enter an anti-Soviet alliance. Russia was the real target, but when these demands were not satisfied the Nazi propaganda machine was wound up and began to emit the old familiar chorus that German minorities were being mistreated and persecuted, this time by the Poles.

British and French Guarantees to Poland

On 31st March 1939 the British Government announced that it would give Poland all the help it could in the event of a German attack. The French followed suit. [See Source 26] Hitler seems to have expected continued efforts to appease him, but he quickly overcame his surprise and accused these powers of building up their armaments and attempting to encircle Germany, a threat against which she would have to defend herself. This time hostile noises did not bring forth offers to negotiate. Instead Britain and France agreed to sign a Mutual Assistance Treaty with Poland. A bill to conscript men of military age for military training was introduced for the first time in peacetime in Britain and began a rapid passage through Parliament. The German response was to renounce the 1934 Anglo-German Naval Agreement.

Italian Annexation of Albania

International tension was raised still further on April 7th by Italy's invasion and annexation of her client state, Albania. Mussolini felt that the climate was right for aggression and that Hitler had staged so many spectacular coups that his own status would be impaired in Italy unless he did something similar.

The Germans were warmly supportive of the Italian action. Although the Albanian adventure had been intended as a demonstration of Italy's independence from Germany, Mussolini found himself more in need of Hitler's support than ever in the face of a hostile reaction from Britain and France. He also knew that Italy was in no condition to fight a big war and needed several years of peace, a fact which made Germany's obvious designs on Poland alarming. The Germans, however, were pressing for a formal military alliance to replace the less binding Axis agreement. Reassured by the improbable promise that Germany also wanted four or five years of peace, Mussolini agreed. In

May 1939 the 'Pact of Steel' was signed whereby each power agreed to come to the aid of the other if it became involved in hostilities "contrary to its wishes and desires".

Despite Hitler's protests against encirclement, Britain's guarantees to Poland meant little in effect. Britain and France were too far away to help Poland if Germany invaded her. The leading statesmen all knew that the most important factor in the months to come would be the attitude of the Russians. Germany would be reluctant to fight Britain, France and Russia again and Poland would be hopelessly isolated if Russia co-operated with Germany. This last scenario seemed unlikely in view of Hitler's well-known distaste for communism.

Anglo-French talks with the USSR

While Hitler and Mussolini were concluding the Pact of Steel, the British and the French opened negotiations with the Russians on 16th April. These talks were pursued, without any great urgency, at ambassadorial level. Britain failed to send a cabinet minister to Moscow and as a result failed to convince the Russians of the seriousness of her intent. It may be that after Stalin's purge of army officers Britain doubted whether Russia, still viewed as a backward and primitive country, could give effective help. Chamberlain wrote to his sister,

"I must confess to the most profound distrust of Russia. I have no belief whatever in her ability to maintain an effective offensive, even if she wanted to. And I distrust her motives, which seem to have little connection with our ideas of liberty ... Moreover, she is hated and suspected by many of the smaller States, notably by Poland, Rumania and Finland."
(Keith Feiling *Neville Chamberlain* quoted by Martin Gilbert in *Britain and Germany Between the Wars* p134)

Britain and France merely wanted Russia to join in the guarantees to Poland but the Russians wanted much more. They proposed a mutual assistance treaty whereby Britain, France and Russia would all agree to come to the aid of any of the other powers if it was attacked. They also wanted precise details of the form this military assistance would take before they agreed to sign a treaty and they required approval for plans to deal with what they called "indirect aggression". They proposed to intervene if any of their neighbours suffered a takeover by local fascist politicians. The British and French saw this as an excuse for the Russians to meddle in the internal affairs of their smaller neighbours and would have nothing to do with it. The western powers have always been deeply suspicious of the messianic aspect of communism. The Russians, for their part, suspected their suitors of trying to promote a war between Russia and Germany which would weaken both to the benefit of the Western powers. The talks staggered on into July but achieved nothing.

RENDEZVOUS

Hitler and Stalin, their long standing and fundamental antagonism momentarily ended by the Nazi-Soviet Pact of August 1939, meet across the dead body of Poland and exchange courtesies.

The Nazi-Soviet Non-Aggression Pact

Russia had in fact made overtures to Germany as early as April 17th, about the time that the talks with Britain and France began. In theory an agreement should have been impossible. Hitler's hatred of communism was second only to his distaste for the Jews. His two phobias were often connected, since in his fantasy world communism was part of a Zionist conspiracy to weaken Germany. He had also advocated that the Germans take 'Lebensraum' in eastern Europe, directly at the expense of the Russians. However, at this stage he had no desire to get involved in a war on two fronts against Britain, France and Russia, the mistake of 1914, and was willing to strike a deal. Stalin, for his part, was deeply suspicious of the French and British governments whose hostility to 'Bolshevism' was a long established phenomenon going back beyond their intervention in the Russian Civil War. He could not see them as real allies and he had seriously weakened the Red Army by his brutal purge of its officer corps. Although it was against the declared ideals and philosophies of both dictators, a deal was very much in the short-term interests of both.

As negotiations between Britain, France and Russia faltered and died, Hitler was able to step in with an offer. On August 23rd 1939 the world was shocked by the signing of the Nazi-Soviet Non-Aggression Pact, on the face of it one of the most cynical treaties ever signed. Its secret clauses provided that Russia would remain neutral if Germany attacked Poland and that Poland would subsequently be partitioned between the two powers. It was the sort of treaty despotic kings made in the eighteenth century. Poland's end could not now be far away.

Once the Pact had been signed, Hitler set about attempting to isolate Poland from her western allies. On August 25th he offered to guarantee the British Empire in perpetuity and suggested that once this "last great problem" had been solved he would retire from public life and concentrate on his real life's work, art. However, Chamberlain had lost his capacity to believe Hitler and asked for guarantees of a peaceful settlement with Poland.

Mussolini's need for several years of peace was being totally ignored by Hitler. He was scared to withdraw from the Pact of Steel in case Hitler turned on him, and yet he knew that the Italian army was in no condition to fight a big war. He sent Hitler a message offering moral support in the event of a war over Poland, but regretted that armed support would be impossible unless Germany sent lavish donations of military supplies and raw materials. Hitler then asked for economic and propaganda support but declined Mussolini's offer to sponsor another Munich-style conference.

Hitler's Last Offer to Britain

On Sunday 27th August a new offer from Hitler reached London. The main elements of this were:

- Germany and Britain should make a peace pact.
- Britain should help Germany to secure Danzig and the Polish corridor but Poland would be allowed to use the port of Danzig.
- Germany would guarantee Poland's frontiers.
- Germany should have her colonies, lost in 1919, restored.
- Germans living in Poland would be guaranteed protection.
- Germany would guarantee to protect the British Empire.

Despite Hitler's poor record of keeping promises, this raised some hope in Britain. The Empire did not require German protection, but direct negotiations between Germany and Poland offered some prospects of averting war. Hitler then demanded that a Polish negotiator with full power to make binding agreements be sent to Berlin within twenty four hours. Realising the sort of pressure that would be put on this unfortunate once he got to Germany, Britain rejected this as unreasonable. This charade continued until 31st August when it became obvious that the British were not going to compel the Poles to capitulate.

On 30th August the Germans had made known details of a fairly generous settlement plan. Its purpose may have been to convince the German people that the Führer was doing everything to preserve peace because the next day, before the plan could be discussed or accepted, hostilities against Poland began with an elaborate ruse. SS soldiers, dressed in Polish uniforms, staged an attack on a German radio station near the border. To add authenticity to the scene, they left behind the bodies of a number of convicted criminals who had been dressed in Polish uniforms, killed by lethal injection and then shot. On the following day Hitler drove through a quiet and subdued Berlin to announce in the Reichstag that German troops had been returning Polish fire. Hitler did not expect action from Poland's guarantors. In a memorandum of the time the German Admiral, Bohm recorded,

"In the Führer's view, the probability of the Western Powers intervening in this conflict is not great...When Poland ... asked for arms, they (the British) gave them ludicrous amounts of obsolete material. In other words, the British had refused any real help, saying that they needed the money and the arms for themselves ... It therefore seems out of the question that ... a responsible British statesman will assume the risk of war for his country. France cannot afford a long and bloody war. Its manpower is too small, its supplies are insufficient. France has been pushed into this whole situation against its will..."
(*The Nazi Years* by Remak pp117-118)

Yet on Sunday 3rd September, the British government presented an ultimatum to Germany to call off the attack by 11 am. The French followed suit and soon Europe was at war. When the matter was debated in the South African Parliament, the anti-British Herzog sought to keep his country out of the war. He was defeated by 80 votes to 67 and resigned. Jan Christiaan Smuts, the liberal Boer, became Prime Minister again and led his people to war against Nazism. Before long they were driving the Italians out of Abyssinia . Six years later the war was over and about 54 million people had been killed. Among the dead were Benito Mussolini, Italy's Duce, and Adolf Hitler, Führer and Reich Chancellor of Germany.

Telegram from the British Foreign Secretary to the British Ambassador at Berlin, 3 September 1939, 5 am

Please seek interview with Minister for Foreign Affairs at 9 am today, Sunday, or, if he cannot see you then, arrange to convey at that time to representative of German Government the following communication:

'In the communication which I had the honour to make to you on 1st September I informed you, on the instructions of His Majesty's Principal Secretary of State for Foreign Affairs, that, unless the German Government were prepared to give His Majesty's Government in the United Kingdom satisfactory assurances that the German Government had suspended all aggressive action against Poland and were prepared promptly to withdraw their forces from Polish Territory, His Majesty's Government in the United Kingdom would, without hesitation, fulfil their obligations to Poland.

Although this communication was made more than twenty four hours ago, no reply has been received but German attacks upon Poland have been continued and intensified. I have accordingly the honour to inform you that, unless not later than 11 am, British Summer Time, today 3rd September, satisfactory assurances to the above effect have been given by the German Government and have reached His Majesty's Government in London, a state of war will exist between the two countries as from that hour.'

If the assurance referred to in the above communication is received, you should inform me by any means at your disposal before 11 am today 3rd September. If no such assurance is received here by 11 am, we shall inform the German representative that a state of war exists as from that hour.

German reply to British Ultimatum, 3 September 1939, 11.20 am

The German Government have received the British Government's ultimatum of the 3rd September, 1939. They have the honour to reply as follows:

1 The German Government and the German people refuse to receive, accept, let alone to fulfil, demands in the nature of ultimata made by the British Government.

2 On our eastern frontier there has for many months already reigned a condition of war. Since the time when the Versailles Treaty first tore Germany to pieces, all and every peaceful settlement was refused to all German Governments. The National Socialist Government also has since the year 1933 tried again and again to remove by peaceful negotiations the worst rapes and breaches of justice of this treaty. The British Government have been among those who, by their intransigent attitude, took the chief part in frustrating every practical revision. Without the intervention of the British Government – of this the German Government and German people are fully conscious – a reasonable solution doing justice to both sides would certainly have been found between Germany and Poland. For Germany did not have the intention nor had she raised the demands of annihilating Poland. The Reich demanded only the revision of those articles of the Versailles Treaty which already at the time of the formulation of that dictate had been described by understanding statesmen of all nations as being in the long run unbearable, and therefore impossible for a great nation and also for the entire political and economic interests of Eastern Europe. British statesmen, too, declared the solution in the East which was then forced upon Germany as containing the germ of future wars. To remove this danger was the desire of all German Governments and especially the intention of the new National Socialist People's Government. The blame for having prevented this peaceful revision lies with the British Cabinet policy. ...

5 The German Government, therefore, reject the attempt to force Germany, by means of a demand having the character of an ultimatum, to recall its forces which are lined up for the defence of the Reich, and thereby to accept the old unrest and the old injustice. The threat that, failing this, they will fight Germany in the war, corresponds to the intention proclaimed for years past by numerous British politicians. The German Government and the German people have assured the English people countless times how much they desire an understanding, indeed close friendship, with them. If the British Government hitherto always refused these offers and now answer them with an open threat of war, it is not the fault of the German people and of their Government, but exclusively the fault of the British Cabinet or of those men who for years have been preaching the destruction and extermination of the German people. The German people and their Government do not, like Great Britain, intend to dominate the world, but they are determined to defend their own liberty, their independence, and above all their life. The intention ... of carrying the destruction of the German people even further than was done through the Versailles Treaty is taken note of by us, and we shall therefore answer any aggressive action on the part of England with the same weapons and in the same form.

9 APPEASEMENT : A FINAL PERSPECTIVE

... WITH THE BENEFIT OF HINDSIGHT

The debate on appeasement has continued unabated since the 1930s. Was it realistic? Did it encourage aggression? Was it a policy at all or simply an expression of weakness and gullibility? Did it stem from high-minded principles or did it represent the betrayal of principle? Did Britain, and its government, have any alternative? Did the British government gain anything from the pursuit of that policy?

Below are a few of the contributions which have been made to this debate.

In the thirties the Liberal Party was the most consistently critical of appeasement. Sir Herbert Samuel wrote,

"For some years the Liberal Party had been in almost continuous opposition to the course taken in foreign affairs by the Baldwin-Chamberlain Governments. If they had promoted a policy of removing any grievances, especially economic, of which 'the Have-Not Powers' - Germany, Italy and Japan - might legitimately complain, we should certainly have supported them. ... But such a policy was not promoted. With that which was in fact pursued we disagreed altogether. We disagreed with the cold shouldering of Soviet Russia - the emphasising of points of difference, the refusal to seek a basis of cooperation. We condemned the desertion of the League, the surrender to Italy on Abyssinia, the pusillanimous toleration of German and Italian armed intervention in Spain. We continually criticised the wholly inadequate effort for our own rearmament. From these causes came the impossible situation which this country found itself in at the time of the Munich Conference."
(Viscount Samuel *Memoirs* p275-276)

Sir Archibald Sinclair, the Liberal leader in 1939, succinctly summed up his feelings about the achievements of appeasement,

"We have eaten dirt in vain."
(quoted in Rock *British Appeasement in the 1930s*)

The Labour Party and a growing group of Conservatives, including Winston Churchill, Anthony Eden and Duff Cooper, were equally critical of the policy, but made little impact on either the Government or on public opinion. Appeasement was a popular policy. Sir John Junor, a newspaper editor, recalled in a radio conversation with Charles Kennedy that a bye-election was held in West Aberdeenshire and Kincardine in March 1939, only days after Hitler had dishonoured his Munich pledge and devoured the remaining part of Czechoslovakia. This made the Liberals confident of victory as the Conservative candidate, Thornton Kemsley, had tried to have Churchill deposed from his Epping constituency on the grounds that his opposition to appeasement constituted disloyalty to the party and to Britain. Thornton Kemsley called for the nation to rally behind Chamberlain in that time of trouble. To the amazement of Junor and the Liberals he won.

Appeasement and Chamberlain were also popular in Germany.

"These obviously spontaneous and unorganised ovations for Chamberlain implied a certain criticism of Hitler. When a crowd in an Authoritarian State so demonstratively applauds, not its own god-like dictator, but a foreign statesman from the democratic west with an unheroic umbrella, this constitutes a very definite expression of public opinion ... The populace of Berlin and Munich demonstrated in no uncertain manner its aversion to war and its joy at the maintenance of peace."
(Dr Paul Schmidt *Hitler's Interpreter* p113. Quoted by Viscount Simon in *Retrospect*.)

In July 1940, after the fall of France, *Guilty Men*, a scathing attack on appeasement was published in Britain under the pseudonym of 'Cato'. Written by three Liberal and Labour journalists it did not hold back its punches. MacDonald and Baldwin were accused because they "took over a great Empire, supreme in arms and secure in liberty. They conducted it to the edge of annihilation." Baldwin was accused of having overseen "the reduction of British air power to fifth in world rank" and Chamberlain's government "did not exert itself to any great extent in the arming of our country." Cato demanded, "Let the guilty men retire." Chamberlain had already resigned to be replaced by Churchill. The 'Guilty Men' thesis gained widespread acceptance during the war and in the years immediately afterwards.

Writing after the war, Sir Samuel Hoare said in defence of the policy,

"Since the time when Eden first used it with general approval during the debates on the German occupation of the Rhineland in 1936 ... it was a noble word, and at the time seemed to express a wise and humane policy. Appeasement did not mean surrender, nor was it a policy to be only used towards dictators. To Chamberlain it meant the methodical removal of the principal causes of friction in the world."
(Viscount Templewood *Nine Troubled Years* Collins 1954)

Recent historians have been kinder to the 'Guilty Men' than Cato. In many ways they were anticipated by Winston Churchill , perhaps appeasement's most noted critic. In a speech in the House of Commons following Chamberlain's death in 1940, the 'Great Commoner' gave a shrewd appreciation of the advantages which Neville Chamberlain's policy had won for Britain. He also displayed many of the qualities which contributed to his own greatness, not least his generosity of spirit and his magnanimity.

"... It fell to Neville Chamberlain in one of the supreme crises of the world to be contradicted by events, to be disappointed in his hopes, and to be deceived and cheated by a wicked man. But what were these hopes in which he was disappointed? What were these wishes in which he was frustrated? What was that faith that was abused? They were surely among the most noble and benevolent instincts of the human heart - the love of peace, the toil for peace, the strife for peace, the pursuit of peace, even at great peril and certainly to the utter disdain of popularity of clamour. Whatever else history may or may not say about these terrible, tremendous years, we can be sure that Neville Chamberlain acted with perfect sincerity according to his lights and strove to the utmost of his capacity and authority, which were powerful, to save the world from this awful, devastating struggle in which we are now engaged. This alone will stand him in good stead as far as what is called the verdict of history is concerned.

"But it is also a help to our country and to our whole Empire, and to our decent, faithful way of living that, however long the struggle may last, or however dark may be the clouds which overhang our path, no future generations of English-speaking folks - for that is the tribunal to which we appeal - will doubt that, even at a great cost to ourselves in technical preparation, we were guiltless of the bloodshed, terror and misery which have engulfed so many lands and peoples, and yet seek new victims still. Herr Hitler protests with frantic words and gestures that he has only desired peace. What do these ravings and outpourings count before the silence of Neville Chamberlain's tomb? Long and hard, hazardous years lie before us, but at least we entered upon them united and with clean hearts ...

"After he left the Government he refused all honours. He would die like his father, plain Mr Chamberlain." (Rt Hon Winston Churchill, MP *Hansard* 12.11.1940)

the End

This table reveals the extent of the problem of national minorities which existed throughout Europe during the inter-war years

ETHNIC TABLE

(The figures can only be very rough estimates as they obviously varied during the twenty years between 1919 and 1939. Most of the figures derive from census tables of about 1930.)

TOTAL POPULATIONS		MINORITIES	
CZECHOSLOVAKIA	14,700,000	*Germans*	3,250,000
		Czechs: just over	650,000
		Magyars	700,000
		Slovaks: just under	300,000
		Ruthenes	400,000
		Poles (Teschen)	70,000
ESTONIA	1,700,000	*Germans*	17,000
		Russians	170,000
FINLAND	3,600,000	Swedes	300,000
HUNGARY	8,700,000	*Germans*	500,000
ITALY	42,000,000	*Germans*	250,000
		Slovenes and Croats	500,000
LATVIA	(under) 2,000,000	*Germans*	65,000
LITHUANIA	2,500,000	*Germans* (chiefly in Memel-Land)	100,000
POLAND	32,000,000	*Germans*	800,000
		Ukranians and White Russians	6,000,000
		Jews (mostly unassimilated)	3,000,000
ROUMANIA	18,800,000	*Germans*	750,000
		Magyars	1,500,000
		Jews (mostly unassimilated)	700,000
		Ukranians	400,000
		Russians	400,000
		Bulgars	360,000
SWITZERLAND	4,000,000		
German-speaking	2,900,000		
French-speaking	831,000		
Italian-speaking	242,000		
Romantsch-speaking	27,000		
YUGOSLAVIA	14,000,000	*Germans*	500,000
Serbs	5,500,000	Macedonia	600,000
Croats	4,500,000	Magyars	500,000

[From *Europe of the Dictators* p.267/8 by Elizabeth Wiskerman (Fontana/Collins)]

Questions

1 How successful had the framers of the Treaty of Versailles been in implementing the principles of national self-determination?

2 What threat did the Nazi slogan " ein Volk, ein Reich, ein Führer" (one people, one empire, one leader) pose to European peace?

This is a minute by Sir Robert Vansittart, an influential civil servant in the Foreign Office, to Sir Samuel Hoare, the Foreign Secretary, and Anthony Eden, Minister for League of Nations Affairs, dated June 8 1935. For Vansittart's views on appeasement see page 36.

Source 2

I need not comment on this at length, for we have had the meeting. It provided satisfactory material for Mr Eden's speech the next day - but not much material for future policy.

The position is as plain as a pikestaff. Italy will have to be bought off - let us use and face ugly words - in some form or other, or Abyssinia will eventually perish. That might in itself matter less, if it did not mean the League would also perish (and that Italy would simultaneously perform another volte-face into the arms of Germany, a combination of haute politique and haute cocotterie that we can ill afford just now).

I agree that we cannot trade Abyssinia. The price that would now satisfy Italy would be too high for Abyssinia even to contemplate.

If we are all clear and in unison about that, it follows clearly that either there has got to be a disastrous explosion - that will wreck the League and very possibly His Majesty's Government too, if the League is destroyed on the eve of an election - or else that we have got to pay the price ... with British Somaliland, though payment would clearly have to be deferred, even if promised.

Personally I opt unhesitatingly for the latter. I have long thought the distribution of this limited globe quite untenable, and quite unjustifiable. Like fools we made it far worse at Versailles. What has happened in regard to Japan, what is happening in regard to Italy, and what is about to happen in regard to Germany, should surely confirm this view to anyone with political antennae. We are grossly over-landed (and British Somaliland is a real debit.) Indeed, looking a little further ahead - say a couple of generations at most - who can for a moment imagine that Canada and Australia will really be allowed to continue their present policies of shut doors and shut eyes?

I should like to see the question of Somaliland considered at least, while we can still get something for less than nothing. If this cock won't fight, let someone else produce another that will. But whence? Failing these, we may prepare for a horrid autumn - and beyond.

From *Documents in British Foreign Policy* Third Series
Vol. XIV Doc. 301 [HMSO]

Questions
1 What dangers did Vansittart see in the Abyssinia situation?
2 Why was he critical of the Treaty of Versailles?
3 What solution to the problem did he reject and why?
4 What solution did he favour?
5 Was he optimistic that this solution would work?
6 What does this document show about British attitudes to Mussolini's Italy?

A letter from Admiral Sir A Ernle Chatfield to Sir R Vansittart. A senior Admiral and veteran of Jutland reports on the readiness of all three armed services for action over Abyssinia in August 1935.

Source 3

We had an important meeting of the Chiefs of Staff this afternoon to draw up our report as to the measures to be taken at once, and other measures that require Cabinet approval, in view of the Mediterranean situation. I was surprised to find how very unready the other two Services were and how long it would take them before they could give any effective resistance to Italian action by land or air. The Naval situation is bad enough, as you are well aware, and consequently we have put an important covering letter to our Report which it is most necessary that the Secretary of State, Eden and yourself should see before you go to Paris. We also think that the Prime Minister should receive a copy, if possible. Cabinet secretaries will arrange this I think.

Apart from our proposals as to steps to be taken the sense of our feeling is that everything possible should be done to avoid precipitated hostilities with Italy until we are more ready. It would be a serious business if the great League of Nations, having at last agreed to act together, was able to be flouted militarily by the nation whom it was trying to coerce. The Navy will, of course, do its best provided you give us time and enough warning, but it would be a dangerous prospect for us to go to war with Italy with the British Fleet unmobilised and the Home Fleet on leave and scattered. It would indeed be the greatest foolishness if anything of the sort happened.

Further, we are exceedingly anxious lest you should obtain the moral support of France without a definite assurance of her military support also and some knowledge of what that military support would be, which indeed ought to be concerted beforehand in London or Paris. War is not a light measure which we can go into blindfold trusting to luck.

I only want to be sure that the Foreign Office are fully apprised of the military situation and they do all they can to delay the danger of hostilities meanwhile authorising us to prepare. When the meeting at Geneva takes place and if all this is going to happen it would be equally important to obtain the military support of all the Mediterranean Powers as we shall want to use their harbours and to have the assistance of their naval forces. Further, it must not be forgotten that the United States and Germany can completely frustrate Article 16 of the Covenant if they are not approached beforehand and their benevolent neutrality obtained.

From *Documents in British Foreign Policy*
Third Series Vol. XIV. Doc. 431 [HMSO]

Questions
1 Summarise in your own words the main points made by Admiral Chatfield.
2 How accurate and how reliable do you think the content of the Admiral's letter was?
3 If you had been British Foreign Secretary, what policy would you have adopted towards Italy in the light of this letter and 'Source 2'? Give reasons for your answer.

The German Ambassador in Britain reports a conversation with Duff Cooper, a leading opponent of appeasement, two days after the remilitarisation of the Rhineland. This document, and the other German documents used here, was captured by the allies at the end of the Second World War, edited by an international team of scholars, and published in Britain, France and the USA.

Source 4

I had dinner last night with some of my acquaintances from among the circle of political personalities, amongst whom Duff Cooper, the British War Minister, was also present.

In an exhaustive conversation with the Minister, with whom I have been on friendly terms for twenty five years, I asked him about his views on the situation.

Cooper said first of all that he much deplored the way in which we had acted and reproached us with having unilaterally violated a treaty which we had concluded of our own free will; this I refuted, pointing out that France had destroyed Locarno through her alliance with Bolshevism. The Minister then stated that with our offers, whose importance he fully appreciated, we could assuredly have achieved the abolition of demilitarisation by negotiation; this I firmly contested, citing the obstinacy of the French. But I again had the impression that, as other signs have of late also seemed to me to indicate, the idea of the moral indefensibility of unilateral demilitarisation has become firmly rooted in some British minds.

Cooper then went on to say that, though the British people were prepared to fight for France in the event of a German incursion into French territory, they would not resort to arms on account of the recent occupation of the German Rhineland. The people did not know much about the demilitarisation provisions, and most of them probably took the view that they did not care 'two hoots' about the Germans reoccupying their own territory.

It was of course a different matter where general policy was concerned. Here one could expect opposition from the French, who would not want to accept the 'breach of treaty'. Moreover, as regards the German offers, one would have to expect to hear from all quarters the objections raised that no trust could be placed in fresh obligations undertaken by Germany, now that Germany had broken a treaty which she had concluded of her own free will; as a result, the position was definitely ... (one word missing) and, for the moment, quite unpredictable.

With regard to the atmosphere in Parliament, the Minister said that on the Right many hoped that Germany would be taken at her word and that, in particular, the chance of bringing Germany back into the League of Nations would be seized. Such tendencies also existed on the Left, but they were held in check by opposition to the new Germany. The attitude of the League of Nations Union and of Lord Cecil,[1] which had not yet been ascertained, would probably play its part. I will try to see Cecil tomorrow.

Amongst the other people present, I found several to be warmly in favour of the basic idea of the overall solution for which Germany is striving, coupled, however, with regret over the so-called breach of treaty.

The young Lord Duncannon, who has just arrived from Geneva, and who works in the Secretariat of the League of Nations, informed me that satisfaction was predominantly felt in Geneva and that even Secretary General Avenol had said he hoped that an agreement resulting in Germany's return to the League of Nations could be reached.

HOESCH

[1]Robert, 1st Viscount Cecil, former Conservative Minister, Chairman of the League of Nations Union, a non-official, non-party organisation.

From *Documents in German Foreign Policy*

Questions
1 According to the Ambassador
 (a) Why did Duff Cooper condemn remilitarisation of the Rhineland?
 (b) State fully Duff Cooper's view of British public opinion on the Rhineland.
2 In your opinion, how welcome would this letter be to Hitler and how might it influence the conduct of his policy in this crisis?

On March 25 1936, the German ambassador to Britain reported to the German Foreign Ministry on British public opinion and its possible influence on foreign policy.

Source 5

... It would be wrong to count on this attitude on the part of public opinion, which has so far been so favourable towards us, as a dependable factor in our calculations. Even today it is noticeable that forces are at work to counteract this movement of public opinion towards a frankly pro-German attitude. Whereas during the last few days the familiar opposition to the new Germany and to certain basic principles of her internal policy had receded into the background in comparison with the great international issues, it is now apparent that efforts are being made in a variety of directions to resuscitate this opposition. It is clear that the Opposition are at pains to present their resistance to the idea of military commitments not as a pro-German attitude, but rather as an abstract confession of faith in collective security and against the system of military alliances. Various pronouncements on the Jewish question such as Winston Churchill's outburst yesterday in the House of Commons and the occasional references to the Thälmann case, show that the anti-German forces are endeavouring to attack public opinion at a very vulnerable spot.

The extremely difficult position in which the British Government find themselves, between pressure from France on the one side and that of public opinion on the other, is beginning to cause the many thoughtful Britons serious concern ...

France's resounding failure, both within the Locarno circle and in the Council of the League of Nations, is beginning to cause grave and widespread anxiety here. Uneasiness is felt over the possibility that the Anglo-French rift may widen. France is known to take such failures ill and there are fears for the future of the collective system of safeguarding peace. On the other hand, no one doubts that the French Government will most determinedly insist on the promises given by Britain with regard to future military commitments being fulfilled. In these circumstances people shrink from allowing further inflammable material to be introduced into Anglo-French relations.

For all these reasons we must be prepared to see public opinion become more and more restrained in its inclination to sympathise with the German view and, furthermore, to find criticism of the German action becoming more articulate again.

HOESCH

(From Documents in German Foreign Policy)

Questions
1 What evidence is there in the source to suggest that British public opinion towards Germany might not continue to be so favourable?
2 Why does the ambassador think that the Anglo-French rift might affect Germany in an adverse way?

After the resignation of Hoare over Abyssinia, Eden became British Foreign Secretary. Eventually he resigned from Chamberlain's government over the policy of appeasement. This is an extract from a memorandum written by Eden on the Locarno Treaty.

Source 6

FOREIGN OFFICE, *March 8, 1936*

... 4 The German Government, by the reoccupation of the zone effected on the morning of the 7th March, have thus not by that action produced a result, so far as the demilitarised zone itself is concerned, which we were not prepared ultimately to contemplate. It is the manner of their action, as I informed the German Ambassador yesterday, which we deplore. Herr Hitler might have demanded arbitration as to the compatibility of the Franco-Soviet Treaty with Locarno and awaited the result. This would have been the right course and, indeed, M. Flandin had already offered to follow it. He might have declared himself no longer bound by Locarno, and asked for negotiations to replace it by another treaty without the demilitarised zone provision. This would have been plausible, although contrary to the terms of the treaty. He has chosen, however, to eliminate all negotiations by *reoccupying* the zone at once. It is this which is so highly provocative and puts Herr Hitler entirely in the wrong. He has evidently taken this extreme course (*vide* Berlin telegrams Nos. 51 and 54) against military advice and under the pressure of General Göring and the Nazi extremists. Among his motives was probably the fact that he wished to act before British rearmament brought renewed confidence to the French and increased vigour to the League. He may also have wished to act while Italy was still at issue with the League and with her Locarno partners ...

Future Policy of His Majesty's Government

21 The myth is now exploded that Herr Hitler only repudiates treaties imposed on Germany by force. We must be prepared for him to repudiate any treaty even if freely negotiated (*a*) when it becomes inconvenient; and (*b*) when Germany is sufficiently strong and the circumstances are otherwise favourable for doing so.

22 On the other hand, owing to Germany's material strength and power of mischief in Europe, it is in our interest to conclude with her as far-reaching and enduring a settlement as possible whilst Herr Hitler is still in the mood to do so. But on entering upon this policy we must bear in mind that, whatever time limits may be laid down in such a settlement, Herr Hitler's signature can only be considered as valid under the conditions specified above ...

28 We must discourage any military action by France against Germany. A possible course which might have its advocates would be for the Locarno signatories to call upon Germany to evacuate the Rhineland. It is difficult now to suppose that Herr Hitler could agree to such a demand, and it certainly should not be made unless the Powers, who made it, were prepared to enforce it by military action. Fortunately, M. Flandin has said that France will not act alone (ie. under paragraph 3 of article 4 of Locarno), but will take the matter to the Council (ie. under paragraph 2 of article 4 of Locarno). This he must be encouraged to do. But we must beware lest the French public, if further irritated or frightened, get restless at such a slow and indecisive action and demand retaliatory action of a military character such, for instance, as the reoccupation of the Saar. Such a development must be avoided if possible.

29 While we obviously cannot object to the Council adopting, under article 4(2) of Locarno, a 'finding' that Germany has violated the demilitarised zone provisions, this ought to be on the distinct understanding that it is not to be followed by a French attack on Germany and a request for our armed assistance under that article. An understanding, therefore, as to procedure at the Council between the Locarno Powers is essential before the Council meets, and arrangements are being made to this end.

30 We must be ready at the Council to offer the French some satisfaction in return for their acquiescence in this tearing up of articles 42 and 43 of Versailles and the whole of Locarno ...

34 It will be essential, under present conditions, to do something to steady the situation, and I propose accordingly, and as an immediate step, that a statement should be made in the House tomorrow to the following effect:
'His Majesty's Government regard themselves, during the consideration, which will obviously be necessary, of the situation created by the German denunciation of the treaty, as still in honour bound to come to the assistance of France or Belgium in the event of an actual attack on them by Germany, which would constitute a violation of article 2 of Locarno, and to the assistance of Germany in the event of such an attack upon her by France or Belgium.

(From Documents in British Foreign Policy)

Source 7

Mr Nigel Law had been a senior civil servant in the Foreign Office before going to work in 'the City'. His letter to Moley, Mr Orme Sargent, a former colleague, reveals much about the attitude of British financiers to Hitler.

March 9, 1936

My dear Moley,

The sentiment of the City is overwhelmingly pro-German. No doubt you expected as much. I confess I had never realised before the depth of anti-French feeling which forms the background of all foreign political judgments here. Naturally there are many degrees of this sentiment. The most extreme are the *Daily Mail* readers, who ... are now content to repeat the parrot-cry of 'You can't keep down for ever a nation of 67 million' ... Next come those who disregard the denunciation of Locarno and affirm the right of Germany to reoccupy the demilitarised zone. They look hopefully towards a new era in Europe based on an acceptance of Hitler's offer

... The above are the first reactions of the City ... It does not follow that these are the reactions of the country at large. I have seen too often the extent the views of the City differ from those of the country on foreign affairs to suppose that on this occasion they are identical ... You must remember that

the City always minimises dangers at first because the financial wish is often the father of the political thought. Consequently it concentrates its attention on Hitler's new promises and chooses to forget the breaches of past ones.
Yours ever,
    NIGEL
(From *Documents in British Foreign Policy*)

Source 8

A report by the heads of the three armed services on their ability to fight a war against Germany in 1936.

In view of the gravity of the position resulting from the German occupation of the Demilitarised Zone, we met on the 12th March, 1936, without instructions but with the knowledge and approval of the Prime Minister, to examine the military aspects of the situation. We subsequently directed the Joint Planning Sub-Committee to review the condition of our forces and to render a Report at once on the existing position of our defence forces at Home and the possible improvements which could be achieved by mobilisation either with or without at the same time being relieved of our present extra responsibilities in the Mediterranean. Their Report, as amended and approved by us, is attached to this Memorandum.

2   We realise that the main object of the Government's policy is to avoid any risk of war with Germany. In case, however, there is the smallest risk, either now or later in the negotiations, that we might be drawn into such a war, we wish to offer the following observations.

3   The attached Report gives the facts regarding the forces at our disposal in certain circumstances, and we would at once emphasise, as is obvious from those facts, that any question of war with Germany while we were as at present heavily committed to the possibility of hostilities in the Mediterranean would be thoroughly dangerous. As regards naval operation against Germany, our minimum requirements could only be carried out by weakening naval forces in the Mediterranean to an extent which would jeopardise our position there vis-à-vis Italy. Even so, there would not be sufficient naval forces available to ensure that we could safeguard our coasts or trade against serious depredations of the German Fleet, small as it is. As regards the Army and the Air Force, the purely defensive provisions already made in the Mediterranean have drawn upon the resources of these two Services to such an extent that until those reinforcements have returned to this country we should be quite incapable of dispatching a Field Force or providing any proper defence in the air. To bring home these forces with their equipment, reserves of ammunition and the like would take in the case of the Army two months after the orders for withdrawal are given, and even longer in the case of the Air Force.

4 We also draw attention to the fact that the provision of equipment for the defence of our coasts and ports at Home has to date, with the consent of the Government, been placed in the lowest category of importance, and it is only with the approval of the new programme for the reconditioning of the forces that a serious start is being made to rectify matters in this direction. At the moment our coast defence artillery requires modernisation to a large extent, we have no anti-submarine defences for a number of our most important ports, and the number of our anti-aircraft guns and searchlights is quite inadequate to deal with the air threat from Germany. Even if the reserves of ammunition at present in the Mediterranean were withdrawn, the situation would be little improved ...

6 Therefore, if there is the smallest danger of being drawn into commitments which might lead to war with Germany, we ought at once to disengage ourselves from our present responsibilities in the Mediterranean, which have exhausted practically the whole of our meagre forces. Even then, a considerable period of time must elapse, varying from two to four months as regards the Army and the Air Force, before those forces will be re-established at Home.

7 In the absence of instructions we are not submitting any definite proposals, but we feel that the information in this Memorandum and in the attached Report ought to be available to the Government.

ERNLE CHATFIELD
A A MONTGOMERY-MASSINGBERD
E L ELLINGTON

(From *Documents in British Foreign Policy*)

Questions

1 Explain fully the weakened position of Britain at the time of the Rhineland crisis.
2 What, in your opinion, were the main reasons for Britain's predicament?

This document reveals the feelings of the Wehrmacht (German army) High Command about the advisability of the Rhineland adventure.

Source 9

IMMEDIATE   BERLIN, March 23, 1936
SECRET

For the attention of Geheimrat v. Renthe-Fink.

I enclose herewith data on the armed forces on the German and French sides, together with a map of the area. The data are accompanied by a few comments. The Reich War Minister would be grateful if these could be submitted this morning to the Foreign Minister.

Ambassador v. Ribbentrop has received the same data.

By order:
FRISIUS

SECRET   BERLIN, March 22, 1936
L I a

Military points for the German reply

(1) *The numerical inferiority of the German forces.*
The grand total of troops which have been moved into the former demilitarised zone amounts to about 22,000 men (36,000 including police).
 The troops being held in readiness by France amount, as far as can be computed here, to at least 200,000 men.

(2) *Higher degree of preparedness of the French troops.*
The mass of the French forces is considerably nearer to the frontier than is that of the German troops ...
 The French forces have reached a more advanced stage of mobilisation. They already have at their disposal requisitioned transport etc, and are nearer to their mobilisation areas than are the German troops, who have their peacetime equipment and have moved further away from their mobilisation areas.

(3) *Defensive character of the German forces.*
The German forces which have been moved into the former demilitarised zone are in no way offensive in character.

(From *Documents in German Foreign Policy*)

Questions

1 What does this source reveal about Germany's ability to sustain a military occupation of the Rhineland?
2 Why, in spite of Germany's military inferiority to France, do you think Hitler risked sending troops into the Rhineland?

Jay Allen's report in the *Chicago Tribune* in August 1936 gives a graphic account of the hideous destructive violence of the Spanish Civil War.

Source 10

Right Wing Violence

I know Badajoz. I had been there four times in the last year to do research on a book I am working on and to try to study the operations of the agrarian reform that might have saved the Spanish Republic - a republic that, whatever it is, gave Spain schools and hope, neither of which it had known for centuries.

... thousands of Republicans, Socialist and Communist militiamen and militiawomen were butchered after the fall of Badajoz for the crime of defending their Republic against the onslaught of the Generals and the land-owners.

The Portuguese 'International Police', in defiance of international usage, are turning back scores and hundreds of republican refugees to certain death by Rebel firing squads.

We drove straight to the Plaza. Here yesterday there was a ceremonial, symbolical shooting. Seven leading Republicans of the Popular Front, shot with a band and everything before 3,000 people. To prove that Rebel generals didn't shoot only workers and peasants. There is no favouritism to be shown between the Popular Fronters.

Every other shop seemed to have been wrecked. The conquerors looted as they went. All this week in Badajoz, Portuguese have been buying watches and jewellery for practically nothing. Most shops belong to the Rightists. It is the war tax they pay for salvation, a rebel officer told me grimly. We passed a big dry goods shop that seems to have been through an earthquake. "La Campaña," my friends said. "It belongs to Don Mariano, a leading Azañista. It was sacked yesterday after Mariano was shot."

Suddenly we saw two Falangists halt a strapping fellow in a workman's blouse and hold him while a third pulled back his shirt, baring his right shoulder. The black and blue marks of a rifle butt could be seen. Even after a week they showed. The report was unfavourable. To the bull-ring with him.

We drove out along the walls to the ring in question. Its sandstone walls looked over the fertile valley of Guadiana. It is a fine ring of white plaster and red brick. I saw Juan Belmone, bullfight idol, here once on the eve of the fight, on a night like this, when he came down to watch the bulls brought in. This night the fodder for tomorrow's show was being brought in, too. Files of men, arms in the air.

They were young, mostly peasants in blue blouses, mechanics in jumpers. 'The Reds'. They are still being rounded up. At four o'clock in the morning they are turned out into the ring through the gate by which the initial parade of the bullfight enters. There, machine guns await them.

After the first night the blood was supposed to be palm deep on the far side of the lane. I don't doubt it. Eighteen hundred men - there were women, too - were mowed down there in some twelve hours. There is more blood than you would think in 1,800 bodies.

In a bullfight when the beast or some unlucky horse bleeds copiously, 'wise monkeys' come along and scatter fresh sand. Yet on hot afternoons you smell blood. It is all very invigorating. It was a hot night. There was a smell. I can't describe it, I won't describe it. The 'wise monkeys' will have a lot of work to do to make this ring respectable for a ceremonial slaughter bullfight. As for me, no more bullfights - ever.

We passed a corner.

"Until yesterday there was a pool blackened with blood here," said my friends. "All the loyal military were shot here and their bodies left for days as an example."

They were told to come out, so they rushed out of the house to greet the conquerors and were shot down and their houses looted. The Moors played no favourites.

Back at the Plaza. During the executions here, Mario Pires went off his head. (Mario Pires is a Portuguese correspondent who had been entirely favourable to the Franco Rebellion before his visit to Badajoz.) He had tried to save a pretty fifteen-year-old girl caught with a rifle in her hands. The Moor was adamant. Mario saw her shot. Now he is under medical care in Lisbon.

I know there are horrors on the other side aplenty. Almendra Lejo, Rightist, was crucified, drenched with gasoline, and burned alive. I know people who saw charred bodies. I know that. I know hundreds and even thousands of innocent persons died at the hands of the revengeful masses. But I know who it was who rose to 'save Spain' and so aroused the masses to a defence that is as savage as it is valiant.

"But they didn't burn the jail." I had read in the Lisbon and seville papers that they had. "No, the brothers Plá prevented it." I knew Luis and Carlos Plá, rich young men of good family, who had the best garage in south western Spain. They were Socialists because they said the Socialist Party was the only instrument which could break the power of Spain's feudal masters.

They harangued the crowd that wanted to burn the 300 Rightists in the jail just before they entered, saying they were going to die in defence of our Republic, but they were not assassins. They themselves opened the doors to let these people escape.

"What happened to the Plás?"
"Shot."
"Why?"
No answer.
There is no answer.

Questions
1 What does this source show about the sympathies of the Portuguese officialdom in the Spanish Civil War?
2 Assess this source for bias and reliability.
3 What reasons did Allen give for favouring one side?
4 What excuse does Allen offer for left-wing violence?
5 What does this source tell you about civil wars in general and the Spanish Civil War in particular?

This is an account of the International Brigades by Herbert Matthews, correspondent to the *New York Times*, taken from his book *Two Wars and More to Come*.

Source 11

A leader who is much more expressive of the spirit of the Internationals than any of these is Hans - just Hans, and nothing more. Nobody knows his last name, and nobody asks, for he has relatives in Germany and it would be unhealthy for them if the Nazis learned exactly who Hans was. He is a divisional commander too, who started as the leader of the Thaelmann Battalion of anti-Fascist Germans. If one had to pick out the crack unit of all the Internationals, at least until recently, the choice would have to lie between them and the Garibaldi Battalion of Italians. That is as it should be, considering what Germany and Italy mean in this war.

Hans is thirty eight or thirty nine, married, tall, dark. Before the World War he was a cadet in a military school, for he comes of a good family. During the war he was an officer in the German Army, and he fought well. But what he saw then made him hate nationalism, and he became a journalist for radical newspapers. In the struggle against Hitler he was on the losing side and had to leave Germany.

Thus far his case was that of thousands of refugees. However, he was not content to accept his fate passively. During the Asturian revolt here in 1934, Hans came to Spain to help the miners, who were suppressed with a ferocity that provided one of the causes for the present division in Spain. So when the Civil War started, Hans had no hesitation. Leaving his wife and his job in France, he came here, as he says, "to defend liberty."

... Gustav Regler, political commissar of the brigade and one of the most popular figures in the International Column. Regler comes of a Catholic family, and as a boy he was educated in a Catholic School. Intelligent and sensitive, he had a long internal struggle in his youth from which he emerged as a free-thinker. Like Lukacz and many of the Internationals, Regler is an author. One of his best-known books is about the Saar - *Under Crossfire*. Being anti-Nazi, he had to flee to France after the plebiscite.

His fellow political commissar, Hans Beimler, also a German, was killed in action back in November. Beimler was a Bavarian, whom the Nazis put in the Dachau concentration camp. In some way he escaped, although his widow is still being kept hostage in Germany. He was the real leader of the German Communists here during his service, and although his job was political commissar of the Thaelmann Battalion, he could not resist the chance to take an active part in the fighting . The spirit that moved him was contagious. One day a group of Internationals had to make a charge that carried them around the dangerously exposed corner of a house. The first who went were shot down in their tracks and lay there dead. The others hung back in dismay. Beimler gathered them about him in the shelter of the house and spoke of ideals, of the things they had come to Spain for, of the uselessness of life for them in a world dominated by the forces for which the insurgents stood. A moment later, with Beimler among them, they swung around that corner and took the objective assigned to them. Shortly afterwards he was killed, and his body was sent to Moscow for burial.

There are so many worth writing about! The Garibaldi Battalion fought so magnificently that its leader, at least, must be mentioned. He was Randolfo Pacciardi - one of the many who were intellectuals, but men of action at the same time. Pacciardi is a lawyer - handsome, cultured, less than middle-aged, with a World War record so fine that he was recommended for the highest award in the Italian Army - the Gold medal. After the war he entered politics, not as a Communist or even as a radical, but as a Republican. The word 'republican' did not mean that he wanted to make Italy into a republic, but it was used as an expression of liberalism and democracy. He formed a war veterans' organisation of men sympathetic with his ideas. In a famous law case that Italo Balbo, now Governor-General of Libya, brought against a Socialist newspaper in Ferrara, Pacciardi successfully defended the newspaper.

It goes without saying that such a man became *persona non grata* when the Fascists took power, and one fine morning he fled to Switzerland an hour or so before the police came for him. As happened with so many of his associates, Switzerland did not welcome him either, and he ended in that haven of political refugees - Paris. There for years he successfully pursued the profession of journalism. He is married; he was earning a good living - and he left everything to fight for Spain, because he felt that it was just and right to do so. The Garibaldi Battalion is now dissolved and Pacciardi has gone, perhaps to return. He, too, has played his part. Each life is worth a book in itself, and there are thousands of such lives.

Until now I have not even mentioned any Americans, but recently I had a long talk with Hans Amlie, adjutant of the Washington Battalion, who was lying wounded in a room of the hotel-hospital. Amlie is a mining engineer from Montana - "a prospector," he calls himself, who has roamed far over our West, Mexico, South America. He is not a Communist, not a Socialist, knows and cares nothing about politics, except that he hates Fascism as much as any human being could hate it.

The 'Ludlow Massacre' of striking miners occurred when he was twelve years old and it set an indelible stamp on his spirit. It made him a fighter for the underdog, and in his case the underdog was the miner. Although under age, he served through the World War as a sergeant of Marines, and had a good record. Afterwards he studied mining engineering and found himself getting involved deeper and deeper in that struggle for the underdog.

"I've seen many a mine in my career," he told me, "where they sent men down to work where silicosis was inevitable. Two years' work, one year of dying, and no compensation - that was their career. I've always fought for them, and so I lost job after job, for the owners got to know me. And then this war started. It was perfectly natural for me to come to Spain. This is the only place in the world where people like me belong at the moment. Anyone who loves liberty and hates Fascism must come here!"

And then there was Oliver Law, a Texas Negro, and commander of the Lincoln Battalion after Martin Hourihan was promoted to regimental commander. In the same action that Hourihan got his wounds, although a few days later, Law was killed. A Negro commander of 150 white men who were proud to serve under him - does that not convey something of the spirit of the Internationals? Law was in some sense the typical Negro radical. Sensitive and rebellious against the fate of his people in the South, he naturally drifted into the movement. First, however, he received military training in the American Army, which he joined in Texas after the World War (he was only about thirty-three when he was killed).

His service completed, he went to Chicago, where he was when this war started. In the interim he had become a Communist and an important figure in Chicago's Negro world. A good business-man to boot, he owned a restaurant and other property, which he gave up to come to Spain. And here he died, leading his men in an attack. "We are here to show that Negroes know how to fight Fascists," he said one day of himself and others of his race in the American battalions.

From *Two Wars and More to Come* by Herbert Mathews (J B Lippincott 1938) Reprinted in *The Civil War In Spain 1936-1939* by Robert Payne (Secker and Warburg)

Questions
1 Examine the account of each of the characters in the source and write a short description of their motives for joining the Brigade. Also describe the motives of the Scotish volunteers described in the main text. (pages 30 & 31)
2 In your opinion, what qualities did these volunteers have in common?

'Source 12A' is an account by a Basque priest, Father de Onaindia. This can be contrasted with 'Source 12B' by Peter Kemp, an English anti-communist, who fought for the Nationalists in a Carlist Requeté.

Source 12A

GUERNICA

Late in the afternoon of April 26th I was going by car to rescue my mother and my sisters, then living in Marquina, a town about to fall into the hands of Franco. It was one of those magnificently clear days, the sky soft and serene. We reached the outskirts of Guernica just before five o'clock. The streets were busy with the traffic of market day. Suddenly we heard the siren, and trembled. People were running about in all directions, abandoning every-thing they possessed, some hurrying into the shelters, others running into the hills. Soon an enemy aeroplane appeared over Guernica. A peasant was passing by. "It's nothing, only one of the 'white' ones." he said. "He'll drop a few bombs, and then he'll go away." The Basques had learned to distinguish between the twin-engined 'whites' and the three-engined 'blacks'. The 'white' aeroplane made a reconnaissance over the town, and when he was directly over the centre he dropped three bombs. Immediately afterwards he saw a squadron of seven planes followed a little later by six more, and this in turn by a third squadron of five more. All of them were Junkers. Meanwhile, Guernica was seized with a terrible panic.

I left the car by the side of the road and took refuge with five milicianos in a sewer. The water came up to our ankles. From our hiding-place we could see everything that happened without being seen. The aeroplanes came low, flying at two hundred metres. As soon as we could leave our shelter, we ran into the woods, hoping to put a safe distance between us and the enemy. But the airmen saw us and went after us. The leaves hid us. As they did not know exactly where we were they aimed their machine-guns in the direction they thought we were travelling. We heard the bullets ripping through branches, and the sinister sound of splintering wood. The milicianos and I followed the flight patterns of the aeroplanes; and we made a crazy journey through the trees, trying to avoid them. Meanwhile women, children and old men were falling in heaps, like flies, and every-where we saw lakes of blood.

I saw an old peasant standing alone in a field: a machine-gun bullet killed him. For more than an hour these eighteen planes, never more than a few hundred metres in altitude, dropped bomb after bomb on Guernica. The sound of the explosions and of the crumbling houses cannot be imagined. Always they traced on the air the same tragic flight pattern, as they flew over all the streets of Guernica. Bombs fell by thousands. Later we saw the bomb craters. Some were sixteen metres in diameter and eight metres deep.

The aeroplanes left around seven o'clock, and then there came another wave of them, this time flying at an immense altitude. They were dropping incendiary bombs on our martyred city. The new bombardment lasted thirty five minutes, sufficient to trans-form the town into an enormous furnace. Even then I realized the terrible purpose of this new act of vandalism. They were dropping incendiary bombs to try to convince the world that the Basques had fired their own city.

The destruction of Guernica went on altogether for two hours and forty five minutes. When the bombing was over, the people left their shelters. I saw no one crying. Stupor was written on all their faces. Eyes fixed on Guernica, we were completely incapable of believing what we saw.

Towards dusk we could see no more than five hundred metres. Everywhere there were flames and thick black smoke. Around me people were praying and some stretched out their arms in the form of a cross, imploring mercy from Heaven.

Soon firemen arrived from Bilbao and started to work on some of the buildings which had not been bombed. We heard that the glow of the flames had been seen from Lequeitio, twenty two kilo-metres away. Not even the people who went into the refuges were saved; nor the sick and wounded in the hospitals. Guernica had no anti-aircraft guns, no batteries of any kind; nor were there any machine-guns.

During the first hours of the night it was a most horrifying spectacle: men, women, and children were wandering through the woods in search of their loved ones. In most cases they found only their bullet-riddled bodies.

The buildings near the Tree of Guernica, which stands on a small hill, were unharmed, but the City Hall with its valuable archives and documents was completely destroyed.

When it grew dark the flames of Guernica were reaching to the sky, and the clouds took on the colour of blood, and our faces too shone with the colour of blood.

Father Onaindia left and returned some hours later with his mother and sisters.

We came up in lorries, but when we came to Guernica we knew

62

we would have to abandon them. We could not take the lorries through the flames. We jumped out and made our way through the flames. We jumped out and made our way through the town as well as we could, dodging the flames.

The flames were everywhere. The whole town was burning. Army ambulances were coming up from Bilbao. Men and women were still digging out the bodies. Around the main square every other building had collapsed. The church had been bombed, but the facade was still standing. The convent was destroyed, but there were nuns everywhere, working to help the wounded. Strangely, the tree of Guernica, which is a little way behind the church, was still standing. The tree is in a stone courtyard, with stone benches arranged around it, but the whole courtyard had been spared.

Except for the roaring of the flames, there was no sound. No one spoke, and even the oxen, wandering aimlessly around the town, were silent. Everyone was stunned.

I knew Guernica well, but it was unrecognisable. It is a small town of red roofs and whitewashed walls, very clean. On market days people come from miles around to trade donkeys and cows and dairy produce. Market days were happy days. People sat around and bargained and drank wine and sang. There was no singing. There were dead animals burning in the street. They were digging into the rubble, and removing the charred bodies in ox-carts and taking them to the cemetery.

[Quoted in *The Civil War in Spain 1936-1939* by Robert Payne Published by Secker & Warburg]

> **Questions** (Refer to Sources 12A *and* 12B)
>
> **1 What are the essential differences between the two sources?**
> **2 Which version do you believe and why?**
> **3 Why might events like Guernica strengthen the appeasement tendency in the British establishment?**

Source 12B

Guernica - The Nationalist Account

The Republicans were countering the Nationalist offensive against Bilbao with a propaganda offensive of their own; at this time it was concentrated on the famous Guernica incident. It was very cleverly handled, and a great deal of money was spent on it abroad - Botteau was told by his head office that the Republicans spent six hundred thousand pounds in Paris on propaganda about Guernica alone. The story circulated - and widely believed - was that Guernica, an open town, was destroyed by incendiary bombs dropped by Nationalist aircraft; Cardozo was indignant at the success it was having in England. He was in Guernica immediately after its occupation by the Nationalists, and so was able to make a pretty thorough examination. It was clear to him, he said, that the Republicans themselves had set fire to the town before leaving, just as they had burnt Irun, Eibar and Amorebieta in the course of their retreat through the Basque Provinces; he himself had witnessed the burning of Amorebieta. Certainly Guernica was bombed by the Nationalists, but it was not an open town at the time it was bombed; it was packed with Republican troops, and was, in fact, a Divisional Headquarters. After watching the burning of Amorebieta, he had entered it next day, and talked to some of the few inhabitants that were left. Before abandoning the town the *milicianos* had come to their houses and taken all their food and clothing, even what they were wearing so that they were dressed in pieces of sacking; then they had set fire to the town. "We know," these poor people had told Cardozo, "who burned Amorebieta. So we can guess who burned Guernica."

It seems to me that nothing illustrates better the superiority of Republican propaganda over Nationalist than the Republican story about Guernica was given immediate and world-wide publicity, and is still generally believed; whereas the Nationalist case scarcely received a hearing.

From *Mine were of Trouble* by Peter Kemp (p88-89)

The Spanish Civil War as described by Peter Kemp, an English volunteer in the Nationalist army, in his book *Mine were of Trouble*. It should be noted that the Nationalists did not routinely shoot prisoners. For confirmation of this see *Voices from the Spanish Civil War : personal recollections of Scottish Volunteers in Republican Spain* by Ian Macdougall.

Source 13

Some Allegations of Priest Killing

With the villagers we were on excellent terms. They would often invite us into their houses - the few that remained - for a meal or a glass of wine. From them I learned what had happened to the village priest. In August *milicianos* had come to Santa Olalla from Madrid - strangers to the place. After shooting a number of prominent villagers they crucified the priest in front of the rest. The villagers, who were fond of him, would have saved him if they could; but they were powerless before this armed rabble. "At Alcabón, five kilometres from here," they told me, "the *milicianos* burnt the priest alive." From all I have been able to find out it seems that a very large number, if not the majority, of such atrocities were committed by armed bands who came into the countryside from the large towns, rather than by local peasants ...

We went to report to the Company Commander, whose name, if I remember rightly, was Santo Domingo. We found him in his dugout with another captain, called Frejo, and Father Vicente, the Company Chaplain, a stern-faced, lean Navarrese with the eyes of a fanatic gleaming behind his glasses. Captain Santo Domingo had a great reputation as a soldier in this *tercio* , and was greatly beloved by his men, whom he led by the sheer force of his own example. He was a man of about fortyfive with a strong, gentle face, full of character. Father Vicente, in great spirits, dominated the gathering. He was the most fearless and the most bloodthirsty man I ever met in Spain; he would, I think have made a better soldier than priest.

"*Holám* , Don Pedro!" he shouted to me. "So you've come to kill some Reds! Congratulations! Be sure you kill plenty!" The purple tassel of his beret swung in the candle-light. Santo Domingo frowned:

"Father Vicente, you are always talking of killing. Such sentiments do not come well from a priest. The Reds may be our enemies, but remember they are Spaniards, and Spain will have need of men after the war."

"Of good men, yes. But not of evil."

"Of good men," repeated Santo Domingo, "and of evil men converted."

I was fascinated, as the argument became heated, to see the rôles of the priest and soldier reversed; but I noticed that Father Vicente was alone among the party in his condemnation of all Reds as traitors who must be killed. He needn't worry, I thought, we'll have to kill all we can tomorrow, if only to save our own skins.

Captain Frejo spoke: "It will be hard battle tomorrow; they must outnumber us by at least ten to one. We have no other defences to fall back on, and if we break the whole Jarama front will fold up."

"God will not desert us," pronounced Father Vicente.

The bombardment was reaching a climax. Our ears were throbbing with the explosions, our eyes almost blinded with dust; not so blinded, however, that we could not see that the enemy was getting closer, finding his way surely round to our left flank. Bullets from his light machine-guns were slapping against the parapets and whistling by our heads. Sometimes a Requeté, carried away by excitement, would clamber up on the parapet, half out of the trench, to get a better shot; in a moment he would slump back, torn with bullets, or fall forward over the parapet to roll a few yards down the slope in front. Whenever the latter happened - and I personally saw it happen several times - Father Vicente would leap from the trench and run down the hill to where the body lay, the purple tassel of his scarlet beret flying in the wind; there he would kneel, oblivious to the bullets churning the earth around them, while he prayed over the dead or dying man.

The Treatment of Foreign Prisoners (P162-170)

Once again I found myself tripping and stumbling over wire, but the fighting was finished before we reached the trenches. Beyond were several half-ruined shepherds' huts; against their walls about a dozen prisoners were huddled together, while some of our tank crews stood in front of them loading rifles. As I approached there was a series of shots, and the prisoners slumped to the ground.

"My God!" I said to Cancela, feeling slightly sick. "What do they think they're doing, shooting those prisoners?"

Cancela looked at me. "They're from the International Brigades," he said grimly.

"We shall be opening fire on that monastery soon."

"Well, let's hope you make good shooting," we answered; "we've got to take it"

"I don't think you need worry. By the time the guns and aeroplanes have finished there won't be much resistance left."

...For the next ninety minutes our view of the monastery was hidden in a pall of smoke and dust; no sooner had one bomber squadron dropped its load than another would approach the target, while all the time the guns kept up their fire. At the end it seemed impossible that anyone could be left alive on that hill or, if they were, that they could still be capable of fighting.

By now the Bandera had overrun the whole position; legionaries were moving among the trenches, dispatching with rifle butt and bayonet the few remaining defenders. The enemy were Germans from the Thälmann Brigade, good soldiers and desperate fighters, since even their homeland was barred to them. They expected no mercy and received none; I felt a sickening disgust as I watched the legionaries probe among the fallen, shooting the wounded as they lay gasping for water. I resolved to speak to Cancela at the first opportunity; I had not come to Spain for this. We had in our

Company a German lance-corporal, known as Egon; I never knew his surname, for he was not in my platoon. He was a very young, quiet boy, with a baby face, fresh complexion and innocent light-blue eyes; he was not very popular with his fellows. Reporting for orders I found Cancela interrogating a prisoner; Egon was interpreting. When he had finished Cancela looked at the legionaries around him, then motioned the prisoner away, saying "*A fusilarle*". Egon's face became suffused with excitement: "Please let me shoot him, sir," he begged. "Please let me do it!" His eyes were shining and a small droplet of spittle trickled down his chin. Cancela seemed surprised, but he told Egon to take the prisoner away. Trembling with excitement Egon jabbed his rifle into the prisoner's ribs, barking at him in German: "About turn! Start walking!" They had gone a dozen paces when the prisoner suddenly bent double and started to run, zigzagging as he went. In that flat country he had no chance. Egon fired two or three shots after him; then the legionaries around joined in; within a few seconds the fugitive lurched and fell to the ground. Egon ran to him and fired a couple of shots into his head. He seemed a little disappointed.

I thought it better to defer my discussion with Cancela on the shooting of prisoners to a more favourable occasion.

The Guardia de Asalto, were especially detested by the Nationalists; few of their officers who were taken prisoner survived. Addressing Cancela, de Mora said:

"The Colonel wants some men to shoot this prisoner."

There was a wild scramble around me as a dozen legionaries leaped to their feet, clamouring for the job with an eagerness surprising in men who a moment earlier had seemed exhausted. Even Peñaredonda was startled.

"Quiet, my children, quiet!" he urged in a pained voice. "There's nothing to get excited about. This is simply a creature who is about to pass over to the other side." His unctuous tone barely veiled his satisfaction. He turned to de Mora:

"I think we'd better have an officer." De Mora caught sight of Torres. "Will you undertake it?" he asked. Poor Torres, still suffering from his tonsils, turned a shade paler.

When the prisoner had made his confession to our padre, Torres pulled himself together and, with obvious reluctance, approached the man; they spoke together for a moment; then they walked slowly towards the edge of the escarpment, the escort following. The prisoner stood with his back to us on the top of the bluff, gazing across the shadowed valley to the further side where the slanting sunlight touched the hills with gold. Torres stepped back, drew his pistol and shot him once throught the back of the head.

It was over lunch next day that I nerved myself to ask Cancela:

"Where do the orders come from that we must shoot all prisoners of the International Brigades?"

"As far as we're concerned, from Colonel Peñaredonda. But we all think the same way ourselves. Look here, Peter" he went on with a sudden vehemence, "it's all very well for you to talk about International Law and the rights of prisoners! You're not a Spaniard. You haven't seen your country devastated, your family and friends murdered in a civil war that would have ended

eighteen months ago but for the intervention of these foreigners. I know we have help now from Germans and Italians. But you know as well as I do that this war would have been over by the end of 1936, when we were at the gates of Madrid, but for the International Brigades. At that time we had no foreign help. What is it to us if they do have their ideals? Whether they know it or not, they are simply the tools of the Communists and they have come to Spain to destroy our country! What do they care about the ruin they have made here? Why then should we bother about their lives when we catch them? It will take years to put right the harm they've done to Spain!"

He paused for breath, then went on: "Another thing; I mean no offence to you personally, Peter, but I believe that all Spaniards - even those fighting against us - wish that this war could have been settled one way or another by Spaniards alone. We never wanted our country to become a battleground for foreign powers. What do you think would happen to you if you were taken prisoner by the Reds? You would be lucky if they only shot you!"

Torres's quiet voice interrupted: "If it comes to that, what chance would any legionary stand if he were to fall into their hands, especially into the hands of the International Brigades? We knew what they did to their prisoners at Brunete and Teruel."

"We realize you can't feel the same as we do," concluded Cancela, "but please, Peter, do not speak to me of this again."

Nevertheless, I knew this was not the policy of the Nationalist High Command, who already held several thousand International Brigade prisoners in a camp at Miranda de Ebro, and who released all of them a few months later. Spanish prisoners, of course, were decently treated by the Nationalists at this stage of the war, with the exception of regular officers of the armed forces, who were regarded, by a curious process of thought, as traitors.

For myself, if I were taken prisoner, I expected no mercy.

Questions
1 **What do these sources tell you about the church and its role in the war?**
2 **Describe in detail how the Nationalists treated their prisoners in the incidents described in Source 13.**
3 **How did Cancela justify the shooting of prisoners?**
4 **Do you think Cancela's claims are accurate?**
5 **Is Kemp likely to be reliable in this instance?**
6 **What does this extract tell you about the passions aroused by civil wars?**

If the Germans had invaded Britain, the Gestapo would certainly have arrested David Low, a New Zealander, many of whose cartoons offended the Führer. Low struck his targets time and time again with clinical accuracy. This extract comes from his autobiography.

The bannings of my cartoons in Germany and Italy cut both ways. Although they nipped in the bud my sparse circulation inside the German Reich and Italy, the advertisement did me more good than harm elsewhere, for reprintings in foreign newspapers began to increase and went on until I had quite a respectable regular syndication throughout non-totalitarian Europe and Asia.

German Foreign Office documents published after the war revealed how the Nazis took criticism by the British Press in the prewar years. They complained repeatedly to Lord Halifax, then Foreign Secretary ...

Towards the close of 1937 Lord Halifax visited Germany, ostensibly to see the International Hunting Exhibition in Berlin but mainly to talk to Hitler and advance the prospects of keeping the peace in Europe.

On his return he met Brigadier (then Captain) Michael Wardell, chairman of the *Evening Standard*, and spoke of the intense bitterness among the Nazi bosses over attacks on them in the British Press. Halifax said Hitler and the others were particularly sensitive to my cartoons. Every Low cartoon attacking Hitler was taken to the Führer at once – and he blew up.

Wardell suggested that Lord Halifax should tell me these things personally. Halifax agreed. The meeting took the form of a lunch at Wardell's flat in Albion Gate, where we three had a pleasant and interesting luncheon.

Lord Halifax described the Nazi point of view, explaining that, partly because they had no long tradition of government, the Nazis were unable to take press criticism calmly. He drew verbally a pretty picture of Goebbels raging over a selection of my cartoons laid out in a row on a table. He said the fury and bitterness caused by the *Evening Standard* cartoons was "out of all proportion to the motive which prompted their publication."

Lord Halifax, I knew, was a good man, an upright man. He looked worried and I felt respect and warm sympathy for one who was sincerely striving for peace under the most discouraging circumstances. At the same time, although I did not say it, I felt in my bones that Lord Halifax was not quite the right person to deal successfully with persons whose conceptions of goodness and uprightness were the opposite of his own.

I said something about my having a duty, too, like any other journalist in a democracy whose work had an educative element, to present faithfully the substance of what was happening. I added that although I could understand that the Nazis might find criticism mighty inconvenient, I had difficulty in believing they were so volatile that politeness would cause them to modify their plans. "Do I understand you to say that you would find it easier to promote peace if my cartoons did not irritate the Nazi leaders personally?" I asked, finally.

"Yes", he replied.

We left it at that, and sitting on Wardell's roof-garden we looked at Hyde Park below and talked about the weather.

I had my private sources of information, British and American correspondents travelling to and fro between Britain and Germany, Webb-Millar, John Gunther, Raymond Daniel, Ed Keene and others to tell me how Lord Halifax was being taken for a ride; I had just returned from Austria myself and had smelt something on the wind; and Hitler's last published Budget had given him away as being headed for war. But Lord Halifax, after all, was Foreign Secretary with all the strings in hand, and maybe I was wrong. Without relaxing the critical note, I played it in a less personal key. I dropped Mussolini and Hitler and to take their place invented *Muzzler*, a composite character fusing well-known features of both dictators without being identifiable as either.

In Germany, Dr Goebbels followed up his lead to Halifax by a dissertation on humour wherein he told his fellow-countrymen at what they might laugh. He approved of jokes against Jews; communists (and even liberals) were, of course, fair game; but "a joke," says he, " ceases to be a joke when it touches the holiest matters of the national state" – that is to say Hitler, Nazism, the racial state and presumably himself.

One of the most appalling things about those confused days was the sheep-like docility with which well-meaning people followed a lead up the garden path. One expected such brazen nonsense from Goebbels. But it was horrifying to read a little later in the *Church Times*:

"Good taste, one element of which is kindness, forbids joking concerning subjects which are held sacred by others ... I doubt whether Low's cartoons make Mr Chamberlain's appeasement path any easier."

A few weeks after my conversation with Halifax, Nazi troops entered Austria. Halifax was reputed to have been at first incredulous, then amazed. He *had* been taken for a ride. My restraint had been wasted – if indeed I had not by softening protest contributed my mite to a Nazi manoeuvre to weaken Britain morally before this fresh outrage.

I considered that this let me out and I dropped my politeness.

From David Low's Autobiography.

Questions
1 How had Low annoyed Hitler?
2 Who was Lord Halifax and why did he try to persuade Low to exercise restraint?
3 How did Low respond to Halifax's advice? Explain why he responded in this way.
4 Why did he ultimately change his mind?
5 Why did Low think Halifax was unsuited to his job?

Source 15 is a letter from Hitler to Mussolini, sent just prior to the Anschluss justifying Germany's action while attempting to reassure Italy. Source 16 is the Italian response as seen through Ribbentrop's eyes.

MARCH 11, 1938

EXCELLENCY: In a fateful hour I am turning to Your Excellency to inform you of a decision which appears necessary under the circumstances and has already become irrevocable.

((In recent months I have seen, with increasing preoccupation, how a relationship was gradually developing between Austria and Czechoslovakia which, while difficult for us to endure in peacetime, was bound, in case of a war imposed upon Germany, to become a most serious threat to the security of the Reich.

In the course of these understandings [*accordi*] , the Austrian State began gradually to arm all its frontiers with barriers and fortifications. Its purpose could be none other than:

1 to effect the restoration at a specified time;
2 to throw the weight of a mass of at least 20 million men against Germany if necessary.

It is precisely the close bonds between Germany and Italy which, as was to be expected, have exposed our Reich to inevitable attacks.

Incumbent on me is the responsibility not to permit the rise of a situation in Central Europe which, perhaps, might one day lead to serious complications precisely because of our friendship with Italy. This new orientation of the policy of the Austrian State does not, however, reflect in any way the real desire and will of the Austrian people.))

For years the Germans in Austria have been oppressed and mistreated by a regime which lacks any legal basis. The sufferings of innumerable tormented people know no bounds.

Germany alone has so far received 40,000 refugees who had to leave their homeland, although the overwhelming majority of the people of Austria entirely share their ideology and their political views.

With a view to eliminating a tension which was becoming increasingly unbearable, I decided to make a last attempt to reach an agreement with Herr Schuschnigg and definitely establish full equality for all under the law.

During our conversation in Berchtesgaden, ((I called Herr Schuschnigg's attention in a most serious way to the fact that Germany is not disposed:

1 to permit a hostile military power to establish itself at its borders, the more so since such plans are clearly in contradiction to the true wishes of the Austrian people;

2)) I called Herr Schuschnigg's attention to the fact that Germany could no longer tolerate mistreatment of the National-minded majority in Austria by a negligible minority. I myself am a son of this soil. Austria is my homeland, and from the circle of my own relatives I know what oppression and what sufferings the overwhelming majority of these people who embrace Nationalist ideas have to endure.

I called his attention to the fact that it was impossible - this case being in fact without a parallel in the world - for a great power to permit people of common blood, common origin, and common history to be persecuted, mistreated, and deprived of their rights for these very reasons.

Furthermore, I informed Herr Schuschnigg that if the equality of all Germans in Austria were not restored, we should some day be forced to assume the protection of these kinsmen, abandoned by everyone.

My demands were more than moderate.
In fact, according to all principles of reason, right and justice, and even according to the precepts of a formalistic democracy, Herr Schuschnigg and Cabinet should have resigned to make room for a government enjoying the confidence of the people. I did not demand this. I was satisfied with a number of assurances that henceforth, within the framework of the Austrian laws - which, although they had been enacted unjustly, were in force at the present time - all inhabitants of the country were to be treated in the same way, receive the same privileges or be subject to the same restrictions, and, lastly, some security was to be established in the military sphere ((in order that the Austrian State might not one day become a dependency of Czechoslovakia.))

Herr Schuschnigg made me a solemn promise and concluded an agreement to this effect.

From the very beginning he failed to keep this agreement.

But now he has gone so far as to deal a new blow against the spirit of this agreement by scheduling a so-called plebiscite which actually is a mockery.

The results of this newly planned oppression of the majority of the people are such as were feared.

The Austrian people are now finally rising against the constant oppression, and this will inevitably result in new oppressive measures. Therefore, the representatives of this oppressed people in the Austrian Government as well as in the other bodies have withdrawn.

Since the day before yesterday the country has been approaching closer and closer to a state of anarchy.

In my responsibility as Führer and Chancellor of the German Reich and likewise as a son of this soil, I can no longer remain passive in the face of these developments.

I am now determined to restore law and order in my homeland and enable the people to decide their own fate according to their judgment in an unmistakable, clear and open manner.

May the Austrian people itself, therefore, forge its own destiny. Whatever the manner may be in which this plebiscite is to be carried out, I now wish solemnly to assure Your Excellency, as the Duce of Fascist Italy.

1 Consider this step only as one of national self-defence and

therefore as an act that any man of character would do in the same way, were he in my position. You too, Excellency, could not act differently if the fate of Italians were at stake, and I as Führer and National Socialist cannot act differently.

2 In a critical hour for Italy I proved to you the steadfastness of my sympathy. Do not doubt that in the future there will be no change in this respect.

3 Whatever the consequences of the coming events may be, I have drawn a definite boundary between Germany and France and now draw one just as definite between Italy and us. It is the Brenner.

This decision will never be questioned or changed. I did not make this decision in 1938, but immediately after the end of the World War, and I never made a secret of it.

I hope that Your Excellency will pardon especially the haste of this letter and the form of this communication. These events occurred unexpectedly for all of us. Nobody had any inkling of the

latest step of Herr Schuschnigg, not even his colleagues in the Government, and until now I had always hoped that perhaps at the last moment a different solution might be possible.

I deeply regret not being able to talk to you personally at this time to tell you everything I feel.

Always in friendship,

Yours,

ADOLF HITLER

(No complete text of this letter has been found in the archives of the German Foreign Ministry. The German copy from which the translation has been made gives the letter as it was published in March 1938. The passages omitted on German insistence when the letter was published have been translated from a copy in Italian which is in the archives of the Italian Foreign Ministry. These passages are enclosed in double parentheses.)

From *Documents in German Foreign Policy* Series D Vol. I Doc. 352 [HMSO]

Source 16

Ribbentrop's interpretation of the Italian response to Hitler's letter.

Memorandum for the Führer

The Counsellor of the Italian Embassy, Count Magistrati, who today called on me for a different reason, informed me of the following:

He had received a telegram from the Italian Foreign Minister, Count Ciano, saying that the Italian Government would greatly welcome publication of the Führer's letter to Mussolini in the German press as well.

I replied to Magistrati that I would be glad to ask the Führer, but that I did not think a belated publication of the letter wise. Count Magistrati then asked whether the Führer would insert into his coming Reichstag speech a passage recognising the Brenner frontier again. Such a public confirmation would be particularly welcome to the Italian Government, since it would be the best corrective for certain tendencies which some people were showing with regard to the Tyrol.

RIBBENTROP

BERLIN, March 17, 1938

From *Documents in German Foreign Policy* Series D Vol. I Doc. 396 [HMSO]

Questions (Using Sources 15 and 16)

1 What claims did Hitler make to justify Anschluss?
2 How reliable do these claims seem to you?
3 How did Hitler attempt to reassure Mussolini?
4 Explain why Hitler would feel it necessary to allay any possible Italian fears before Anschluss.
5 Why did the Italians want Hitler's letter to be published in Germany?

Source 17

This is an extract of a speech by Chamberlain in the House of Commons on the Anschluss, March 14 1938.

It is quite untrue that we have ever given Germany our assent or our encouragement to the effective absorption of Austria into the German Reich. We had, indeed, never refused to recognise the special interest that Germany had in the development of relations between Austria and herself, having regard to the close affinities existing between the two countries. But on every occasion on which any representative of His Majesty's Government had had opportunities to discuss these matters with representatives of the German Government it has always been made plain that His Majesty's Government would strongly disapprove of the application to the solution of these problems of violent methods.

The hard fact is that nothing could have arrested this action by Germany unless we, and others with us, had been prepared to use force to prevent it.

(Hansard)

Questions

1 What does Chamberlain deny?
2 Under what circumstances might Chamberlain have been willing to agree to Anschluss?
3 What measures did Chamberlain say would be needed to reverse Germany's seizure of Austria?
4 What conclusions might Hitler have drawn from this speech and the British reaction to Anschluss?

This is one of the more interesting finds among the captured German documents. It reveals Hitler's plans for attacking Czechoslovakia. **Source 18**

Summary of Führer - General Keitel conversation on April 21.

A. POLITICAL

(1) Idea of strategic attack out of the blue without cause or possibility of justification is rejected. Reason: hostile world opinion which might lead to serious situation. Such measures only justified for elimination of last enemy on the continent.

(2) Action after a period of diplomatic discussions which gradually lead to a crisis and to war.

(3) Lightning action based on an incident (for example the murder of the German Minister in the course of an anti-German demonstration).

B. MILITARY CONCLUSIONS

(1) Preparations to be made for political contingencies 2 and 3. Contingency 2 is undesirable because 'Green' security measures will have been taken.

(2) The loss of time through transport by rail of the bulk of the divisions - which is unavoidable and must be reduced to a minimum - must not be allowed to divert from lightning attack at the time of action.

(3) 'Partial thrusts' toward breaching the defence line at numerous points and in operationally advantageous directions are to be undertaken at once.

These thrusts are to be prepared down to the smallest detail (knowledge of the routes, the objectives, composition of the columns according to tasks allotted them).

Simultaneous attack by land and air forces.

The *Luftwaffe* is to support the individual columns (for instance, dive bombers, sealing off fortification works at the points of penetration; hindering the movement of reserves; destruction of signal communications and thus isolating the garrisons).

(4) The first 4 days of military action are, politically speaking, decisive. In the absence of outstanding military successes, a European crisis is certain to arise. *Faits accomplis* must convince foreign powers of the hopelessness of military intervention; call in allies to the scene (sharing the booty!) ; demoralise 'Green.'

Hence, bridging the period between first penetration of enemy's lines and throwing into action the advancing troops by the determined ruthless advance of a motorised army (for instance through Pi past Pr).[55]

(5) If possible separation of the transport movement 'Red' ['Rot'][56] from 'Green'. A simultaneous deployment of 'Red' might cause "Red" to adopt undesirable measures. On the other hand operation "Red" must at all times be ready to come into action.

C. PROPAGANDA

(1) Leaflets for the conduct of the Germans in 'Green' territory [*Grünland*] .

(2) Leaflets with threats to intimidate the 'Greens'.

[54] Operation 'Green' (Fall Grün) was the German code name for the plan of attack on Czechoslovakia. The word "Grün" is similarly used in the documents merely as the code name for Czechoslovakia.

[55] Presumably meaning "through Pilsen and by-passing Prague."

[56] Operation 'Red' (Fall Rot) was the German code name for the military plan on the western frontier against France in the event of her mobilising against the Reich in defence of Czechoslovakia. Similarly the word 'Rot' is used in the documents merely as the code name for France.

From *Documents in German Foreign Policy* Series D. Vol II. Doc.133 [HMSO]

Questions
1 What was 'Operation Green'?
2 What does it reveal about Hitler's methods of orchestrating and managing a crisis?

These are Henlein's eight demands which became the Programme of the Sudeten German Party during the early stages of the Czech crisis. They were to change later.  **Source 19**

THE EIGHT DEMANDS OF KONRAD HENLEIN ANNOUNCED AT KARLSBAD (April 1938)

1 Restoration of complete equality of German national group with the Czech people;

2 Recognition of the Sudeten German national group as a legal entity for the safeguarding of this position of equality within the State;

3 Confirmation and recognition of the Sudeten German settlement area;

4 Building up of Sudeten German self-government in the Sudeten German settlement area in all branches of public life insofar as questions affecting the interests and affairs of the German national group are involved;

5 Introduction of legal provisions for the protection of those Sudeten German citizens living outside the defined settlement area of their national group;

6. Removal of wrong done to Sudeten German element since the year 1918, and compensation for damage suffered through this wrong;

7. Recognition and enforcement of the principle: German public servants in the German area;

8. Complete freedom to profess adherence to the German element and German ideology.

From *Documents in German Foreign policy* Series D Vol. II Doc 135 [H.M.S.O]

Questions

1 To what extent were the Germans a minority within Czechoslovakia?
2 How far did Henlein go in his demands for the German people within the Sudetenland?
3 What do you think that Henlein meant by "German ideology"? (point 8)

Below are extracts from the German minutes of the meeting between Hitler and Chamberlain at Berchtesgaden on September 15, 1938.

Source 20

Mr Chamberlain mentioned in his introductory remarks that since he had become Prime Minister of Great Britain he had always worked for an Anglo-German *rapprochement* and had always been on the lookout for opportunities to put his intentions into practice. In spite of occasional difficulties in Anglo-German relations, he had nevertheless again and again had the feeling that there was the possibility of strengthening mutual relations by a direct exchange of views. During the last weeks the situation had now become so difficult and grave that the danger of a conflict had seemed to him extremely close.

Quite apart from the Czechoslovak question there were today much greater problems down for discussion and, conscious of this tension, he had therefore undertaken the journey to Germany in order, by means of a direct conversation with the Führer, to attempt to clarify the situation ...

He (the Führer) could definitely state that since his youth he had had the idea of Anglo-German cooperation. The war had come as a great internal spirtitual shock to him. However, he had since 1918 kept the idea of Anglo-German friendship constantly in mind. The reason why he had thus taken up the cause of this friendship was that since his nineteenth year he had developed certain racial ideals within himself, which had caused him immediately at the end of the war to have the *rapprochement* between both nations systematically in view as one of his aims. He had to admit that in recent years this idealistic belief in Anglo-German racial affinity had suffered very severe blows. He would, however, count himself fortunate if he could succeed at the eleventh hour, in spite of all this, in leading back the whole political development into channels laid down by the theories which he had advocated again and again in his speeches and writings for a decade and a half.

The situation was very grave. On the basis of the latest information, 300 fatal casualties and many hundreds of injured were to be expected among the Sudeten Germans. There were entire villages from which the population had fled. In these circumstances a decision must be reached in some way or another within a very short time. In this state of affairs he was obliged to state quite frankly that there would be no point in carrying on a conversation in the manner of previous diplomatic discussions. The long journey which the Prime Minister had made would not have proved worth while if they were to stop short at mere formalities...

He knew that it was impossible to unite all the Germans in Europe. Nor did the German ethnic groups who lived farther away from the Reich expect to be united with the Reich. Besides, he had excluded all questions of this kind which would open up old wounds afresh, and in which the success obtained would be out of all proportion to the weight of the sacrifices made.

Germany, had, nevertheless, put forward a general demand in all clarity. The 10 million Germans who lived in Austria and Czechoslovakia, and whose earnest desire it was to return to the Reich to which they had belonged for a thousand years, must be enabled in all circumstances to return to it. In the case of the 7 million Germans in the Ostmark this demand had been met. The return to the Reich of the 3 million Germans in Czechoslovakia he

(the Führer) would make possible at all costs. He would face any war, and even the risk of a world war, for this. Here the limit had been reached where the rest of the world might do what it liked, he would not yield one single step.

Mr Chamberlain asked in this connection whether the difficulties with Czechoslovakia would then be at an end with the return of 3 million Sudeten Germans to the Reich. The question was being asked in Britain whether this was all that Germany was demanding or whether she was not aiming over and above this at the dismemberment of the Czechoslovak State.

The Führer replied that apart from the demands of the Sudeten Germans similar demands would of course be made by the Poles, Hungarians, and Ukrainians living in Czechoslovakia, which it would be impossible to ignore in the long run, but that he was, of course, not their spokesman.

The Czechoslovak question would then, of course, be the last major problem to be solved. There would indeed still be the Memel question, but here Germany would be satisfied if Lithuania carried out the Memel Statute strictly.

Finally, Germany would, of course, always continue to press her demand for colonies; this was at any rate not a warlike demand. However, it would have to be granted one day, and Germany would never recede from it ...

The British Prime Minister referred to the fact that Great Britain was not interested in the Sudeten German question as such. It was an affair between the Germans (or Sudeten Germans) and the Czechs. Great Britain was only interested in the maintenance of peace.

The British Prime Minister emphasised afresh that when it was a matter of saving human lives all chances must be explored to the very last. He was, therefore, repeating his proposal to bring about a kind of armistice and added that he was prepared to agree to a breathing space of this kind of limited duration.

The Führer replied that an immediate pacification of the Sudeten region could be achieved if the Czech State police were withdrawn and confined to barracs. Furthermore, it seemed to him important - and this in answer to the question as to the further course of the conversations - what attitude Britain was adopting with regard to the Sudeten region. Would Britain agree to the secession of these areas and an alteration in the present constitution of Czechoslovakia, or would she not? If Britain could assent to a separation of this kind, and this could be announced to the world as a fundamental decision of principle, then, no doubt, it would be possible by this means to bring about a large degree of pacification in the regions in question. It was, therefore, a matter of knowing whether Britian was now prepared to assent to the detachment of the Sudeten German districts on the basis of the right of national self-determination, and in this connection he (the Führer) was obliged to observe that this right of self-determination had not just been invented by him in 1938 specially for the Czechoslovak question, but that it had already been brought into being in 1918 in order to create a moral basis for the changes made under the Treaty of

Versailles. The conversations could continue on these lines, but the British Prime Minister must first of all state whether he could accept this basis or not, namely, the secession of the Sudeten German region by virtue of the right of self-determination.

The British Prime Minister expressed his satisfaction that they had now got down to the crux of the matter at last. He was not in a position to make categorical statements for the whole of the British Government. Besides, he was obliged, of course, to consult France and Lord Runciman also. But he could give it as his own personal view that, now that he had heard the Führer's motives and now that he saw the whole situation in a clearer light, he was prepared to ascertain whether his personal opinion was also shared by his colleagues in the Cabinet. He could state personally that he recognised the principle of the detachment of the Sudeten areas. The difficulty seemed to him to lie in the implementation of this principle in actual practice. In these circumstances he wished to return to England in order to report to the Government and secure their approval of his personal attitude. At the same time he was proposing that on both sides they should be perfectly clear in their own minds about the practical methods of implementing this principle for it involved the solution of a whole series of problems of organisation and administration.

The Führer stated that he would gladly spare the British Prime Minister a second journey to Germany, for he was much younger and could undertake journeys of this kind, but he was afraid that if he were to come to England, anti-German demonstration would complicate rather than simplify the situation. But, in order to shorten the Prime Minister's journey somewhat, he was proposing for their next meeting the Lower Rhine district, Cologne or Godesberg.

From *Documents in German Foreign Policy* Series D Vol. II Doc.487 [HMSO]

Questions

1　What do the minutes reveal about Chamberlain's view of his role in the crisis?
2　What does Hitler say about his attitude to the British?
3　Why did Hitler say he wanted a quick decision to be taken on the Sudeten problem?
4　What evidence is there in the source that Hitler appeared to be willing to put limits on the idea of 'ein Volk, ein Reich, ein Führer'?
5　What new demand was posed regarding Czechoslovakia and how far was Hitler willing to go to achieve it?
6　What reassurances did Hitler give Chamberlain?
7　What encouragement could Hitler take from Chamberlain's statement that "Great Britain was not interested in the Sudeten German question as such"?
8　What seemed to be Chamberlain's main concern?
9　What final question did Hitler frame which Chamberlain regarded as the crux of the matter?
10　What steps did Chamberlain have to take before he could give Hitler an answer?
11　Where was the second meeting to take place?

This is from the German minutes of the Godesberg meeting between Hitler and Chamberlain on 22 September, 1938.

Source 21

Mr Chamberlain referred to the situation as it had been at the end of the conversation with the Führer at Berchtesgaden. At that time, after personally recognising the principle of self-determination, he had promised to consult his ministerial colleagues and other statesmen, and to obtain their agreement to this principle. He had succeeded, after laborious negotiations, in persuading not only the British and French Cabinets, but also the Czechoslovak Government to agree in principle to what the Führer had demanded during the last conversation ...

(CHAMBERLAIN THEN OUTLINED HIS PROPOSALS)

The Führer expressed to the British Prime Minister his sincere thanks for his efforts to bring about a peaceful solution of the Czechoslovak problem. Hitherto it had not been quite clear to him what proposal Great Britain and France had submitted to Czechoslovakia, and he therefore asked if the plan just expounded by Mr Chamberlain had been submitted also to the Czechoslovak Government.

When Mr Chamberlain replied in the affirmative, the Führer answered that he was sorry to have to say that this plan could not be maintained. The situation was perfectly clear. It was not a question of doing an injustice to Czechoslovakia, but of redressing a 20-year-old injustice done to the German and other minorities. As a matter of principle, a man who has committed a wrong cannot complain when this is put right again. Czechoslovakia was in fact a purely artificial structure which had been called into being at the time for reasons of political expediency, without regard for the wrongs done to other countries. Three and a half million Germans had been handed over to Czechoslovakia contrary to their immediately expressed wish and in contradiction of all historical traditions. A million Slovaks had likewise been incorporated in this State, although never in history had Slovaks been ruled by Czechs. A large area had been torn from Hungary, so that almost a million Hungarians were living in Czechoslovakia against their will. In addition, in 1920, when Poland was engaged in a struggle against the Bolshevists, Czechoslovakia had annexed the Teschen territory, which meant that some hundred thousand Poles also had been included in this country against their will. That was the genesis of a State which possessed neither history nor tradition nor natural conditions of existence. All other nationalities wanted to get out of Czechoslovakia, and only a few days ago the representatives of Hungary and Poland had told him (the Führer) that in no circumstances would they remain in Czechoslovakia. in the last 20 years the Czechs had not succeeded in winning the sympathies of these foreign nationalities; on the contrary hatred had steadily increased.

In the course of the Berchtesgaden conversation he had already told the British Prime Minister that he was naturally speaking in the first place for the Germans. As a result of the peace treaties he had been obliged to give up so many Germans that his first thought and his first care was naturally for them. It was his duty however to remind the British Prime Minister of the demands of the other nationalities with Czechoslovakia, and added that the latter had the sincere sympathy of the German Reich, and that peace could not be established in Central Europe until the claims of all these nationalities had been settled...

The Führer referred to the present critical stage of the Sudeten German problem. Long delay was impossible. The most important thing was to act quickly. The decision must be made within a few days. The whole world knew that military preparations had been made on both sides of the frontier. These had brought about a situation which demanded a decision one way or another. The solution could result either in a lessening of the tension or in renewed increase of tension with a resulting conflict. He must emphasise that the problem must be finally and completely solved by October 1...

The British Prime Minister replied that he was both disappointed and puzzled at the attitude taken by the Führer. He (Chamberlain) had thought that the Führer, after acceptance of his demand for cession of territory, would then be ready to discuss with him the methods and procedure for putting this demand into effect. He (Chamberlain) had willingly recognised at the first conversation the justification of the Sudeten German demands. The situation could not be saved by autonomy within the Czechoslovak area. Now that he had returned with the agreement of his colleagues in the Cabinet and of the French Cabinet to the principle of cession of territory by Czechoslovakia to Germany, he could rightly say that the Führer had got from him what he had demanded. In order to achieve this, he (Chamberlain) had risked his whole political career. At the time of his first journey to Germany, he had been applauded everywhere, because people in Great Britain had thought that a personal talk with the Führer was the best means for a solution of the problem. Now, however, he was being accused by certain circles in Great Britain of having sold and betrayed Czechoslovakia, of having yielded to the dictators and so on, and on leaving England that morning he had actually been booed. All this would show the Führer the difficulties he had had to overcome, the sacrifices he had to make in order to obtain agreement in principle to the cession of territory. He therefore could not quite understand why his proposals could not be accepted...

He, Chamberlain, had no power to negotiate. He could only report the nonacceptance of his proposals and the counterproposal made by Germany and try to convince his own country of the correctness of his line of action. The Führer had certainly not made his task easier.

The Führer replied that his was no easy task either. The feeling of the German people was such that they would prefer the establishment of a strategic frontier, with the corresponding methods, to negotiation...

From *Documents in German Foreign Policy* Series D Vol. II Doc. 562 [HMSO]

Questions
1 What news was Chamberlain able to bring Hitler at Godesberg?
2 How did Hitler respond to this news?
3 How convincing do you find Hitler's reasons for his change of mind?
4 What new demand did Hitler make?
5 What was Chamberlain's reaction to Hitler's new demand?
6 Would you agree with Chamberlain that the Führer had certainly not made his task easier?
7 What did Chamberlain intend to do on his return to London?

At the height of the crisis Hitler made this inflamed attack on the Czechs and their President, Benes, in the Berlin Sportpalast. (26 September, 1938)

Source 22

This Czech state began with a single lie and the father of this lie was named Benes. This Mr Benes ... appeared in Versailles and ... gave the assurance that there was a Czechoslovak nation. ... the Anglo-Saxon statesmen ... could have established the fact that there is no such thing as a Czechoslovak nation but only Czechs and Slovaks and that the Slovaks did not wish to have anything to do with the Czechs ...
... out of hand three and a half million Germans were taken in violation of their right to self-determination ...
The whole development from the year 1918 up to 1938 showed one thing clearly: Mr Benes was determined slowly to exterminate the German element.

... it also became clear what were the international duties of this state. ... No longer was any secret made of the fact that this State was intended, if necessary, to be employed against Germany. A French Minister for Air, Pierre Cot, has expressed this wish quite soberly: "We need the State," he said, "because from this State German business life and German industry can easily be destroyed with bombs" ... And then Bolshevism uses this State as the gateway through which it can find entry. ... Bolshevism uses that State in order to possess a canal leading into Central Europe.

... In this State of Mr Benes the consequences for the Nationalities have been appalling. I speak only for the Germans. It is they who have the highest death rate of all the German tribes, their poverty in children is the highest, their unemployment is the most frightful.

... Then Mr Benes invented a way to intimidate the Germans in Czechoslovakia: the military occupation of the (Sudeten) districts. ... It was that insolent lie of 21 May – that Germany had mobilised – that now had to serve to cover up Czech mobilisation. What followed you know: an infamous international world-wide agitation."
Germany had not called a man to its colours: ... But Mr Benes adopted the standpoint that, protected by France and by England, one could do anything with Germany with impunity ... And ... behind him stood Soviet Russia.

[After negotiations with Chamberlain at the Berghof and Godesberg]

... Mr Benes began his military subjugation afresh – only with still greater violence. We see the appalling figures: one day 10,000 fugitives, on the next 20,000, a day later, already 37,000 ... and today 214,000. Whole stretches of the countryside were depopulated, villages are burned down, attempts are made to smoke out the Germans with hand-grenades and gas. Mr Benes ... is convinced: "Nothing can happen to me: in the end England and France will stand behind me."

[However] ... in the last resort Mr Benes has seven million Czechs, but here there stands a people of over seventy-five millions.

... I am grateful to Mr Chamberlain for all his efforts. I have assured him that the German people desire nothing else but peace, but I have also told him that I cannot go back behind the limits set to our patience. I have further assured him ... that when this problem is solved there is for Germany no farther territorial problem in Europe. ... when the Czechs have come to terms with their minorities ... , then I have no farther interest in the Czech State. And that is guaranteed to him! We want no Czechs!

... I have made Mr Benes an offer which is nothing more than the carrying into effect of what he himself has promised. The decision now lies in his hands: War or Peace! He will either accept this offer and now at last give the Germans their freedom or we will go and fetch this freedom for ourselves.

Now I go before my people as its first soldier and behind me – that the world should know – there marches a people and a different people from that of 1918!

From *The Speeches of Adolf Hitler* edited by N Baynes pp 1517-1526.

Questions
1 What reasons for demanding the Sudetanland does Hitler give in his speech?
2 What accusation does he make against Czechoslovakia?
3 What guarantee does he offer Czechoslovakia?
4 How much trust could be placed in these guarantees?
5 What do you see as the significance of the last paragraph?

Count Ciano, who was married to Mussolini's daughter Edda, was Italy's Foreign Minister and, as such, deeply involved with the events in Munich. His diary emerged after the war.

Source 23

SEPTEMBER 28, 10 am. Four hours to go before the outbreak of hostilities, when Perth telephones to ask for an interview. I receive him at once. He says, with much emotion, that Chamberlain appeals to the Duce for his friendly intervention in these hours, which he considers the last in which something can be done to save peace and civilisation. He repeats the guarantee already offered by England and France for the return of the Sudetenland. I ask Perth whether I am to regard his *démarche* as an official invitation to the Duce to assume the role of mediator. Yes. In that case there is no time to lose – the offer deserves to be given consideration. I tell Perth to wait for me at the Palazzo Chigi. I go to the Duce. He agrees at once on the impossibility of meeting Chamberlain's request with a flat refusal. He telephones Attolico: 'Go to the Führer and tell him, having first said that in any eventuality I shall be at his side, that I recommend that the commencement of hostilities should be delayed for 24 hours. Meanwhile I undertake to study what can be done to solve the problem.' I go back to the Palazzo Chigi. I inform Perth that hostilities are to begin today and confirm that our place is beside Germany. His face quivers and his eyes are red. When I add that nevertheless the Duce has accepted Chamberlain's request and has proposed a delay of 24 hours, he bursts into a sobbing laugh and rushes off to his Embassy. A little later he asks for another interview. He brings with him a message from Chamberlain to the Duce and a copy of another sent to Hitler: a concrete proposal for a Conference of Four with the task of reaching a radical solution of the Sudeten problem within seven days. It cannot be rejected – by rejecting it Hitler would draw the hatred of the world upon himself and have the sole responsibility for the conflict. Palazzo Venezia – the Duce decides to support the English request, particularly as the Führer has now, at Mussolini's desire, had a phonogram of instructions made. I telephone to Perth, to inform him, and to Attolico, to give him directions. Naturally I cancel the meeting with Ribbentrop and Keitel arranged yesterday.

Blondel too, it transpires from a telephone call, is preparing to make a '*démarche*. Not a hope – it is not our intention that France shall interfere. The whole face of the question would be changed and the Germans would, rightly, smell a rat. I telephone to Perth: 'It transpires that France is preparing to put her oar in. I advise you that any *démarche* by Blondel would simply defeat its own ends. Find a way of preventing it. Our work would be imperilled.' He agrees and undertakes to comply with my request.

3 pm. Attolico telephones that Hitler agrees in principle, making certain reservations of secondary importance. He lays down one condition, however: the presence of Mussolini, which he regards as the sole guarantee. The Duce accepts. We leave at 6 tonight, in order to be in Munich, where the Conference is to take place, at 10.30 in the morning.

I return to the Duce with the American Ambassador, bearing a very tardy message from Roosevelt. I remain alone with the Duce. 'As you see,' he says, 'I am only moderately happy, because, though perhaps at a heavy price, we could have liquidated France and Great Britain for ever. We now have overwhelming proof of this.'

We leave at 6. The unanimous prayers of Italy are with us.

SEPTEMBER 29-30. In the train the Duce is in a very good humour.

... At Kufstein we meet the Führer. We get into his carriage, where spread out on a table are all the maps of the Sudetenland and the western fortifications. He explains the situation: he intends to liquidate Czechoslovakia as she now is, because she immobilises forty of his divisions and ties his hands *vis-à-vis* France. When Czechoslovakia has been, as she must be, deflated, ten divisions will be enough to immobilise her. The Duce listens with concentration. The programme is now fixed: either the Conference is successful in a short time or the solution will take place by force of arms. 'Besides,', adds the Führer, 'the time will come when we shall have to fight side by side against France and

73

England. All the better that it should happen while the Duce and I are at the head of our countries, and still young and full of vigour.'

... After a brief stop at the palace where the Duce and I are staying, we go to the Führerhaus, where the conference is to take place. The others have already arrived and are gathered round a table on which snacks and drinks are set out. The Führer comes half-way down the stairs to meet us and, with the rest of his suite, singles out us, the Italians, by a marked distinction of treatment. Brief, cold handshakes with Daladier and Chamberlain – then the Duce, alone, goes over to a corner of the room where the Nazi leaders surround him. There is a vague sense of embarrassment, particularly on the part of the French. I talk to Daladier, and then to François-Poncet,[1] about trivial things. Then to Chamberlain, who says he wants to talk to the Duce. He thanks him for all that he has already done. But the Duce, coldly, does not take advantage of the opening, and the conversation peters out.

We enter the conference room.

... The discussion develops formally and without very much animation. Chamberlain is inclined to linger over legal points; Daladier defends the cause of the Czechs without much conviction; the Duce prefers to remain silent and sum up and draw conclusions when the others have finished their dissertations.

... The conference is continued in the afternoon and virtually breaks up into little groups which try to work out the various formulas. This permits us to talk with greater confidence, and the ice is broken.

Daladier, particularly, is loquacious in personal conversation. He says that what is happening today is due solely to the pig-headedness of Benes. In the last few months he has repeatedly suggested to Benes that the Sudetens should be given autonomy. That would at least have deferred the present crisis. He grumbles about the French warmongers, who would have liked to push the country into an absurd and indeed impossible war – for France and England would never have been able to do anything really useful for Czechoslovakia, once she was attacked by the forces of the Reich.

The Duce, slightly annoyed by the vaguely parliamentary atmosphere which conferences always produce, moves around the room with his hands in his pockets and a rather distracted air. Every now and then he joins in the search for a formula. His great spirit, always ahead of events and men, has already absorbed the idea of agreement and, while the others are still wasting their breath over more or less formal problems, he has almost ceased to take any interest. He has already passed on and is meditating other things.

However, he joins in the discussion again, when it turns to the question of including in the agenda the problem of the Polish and Hungarian minorities. The others, without exception, would gladly have said nothing about it. In fact they try to evade its discussion. But when there is a strong will, the strong will always predominates and others coalesce around it. The problem is discussed and solved by means of a formula which I do not hesitate to describe as very brilliant.

... At last, at one in the morning, the document is completed. Everybody is satisfied, even the French – even the Czechs, according to what Daladier tells me. François-Poncet has a moment of shame while he is collating the document. 'Voilà comme la France traite ses seuls allies qui lui étaient restes fidèles,' he exclaims.

We sign, shake hands, and depart.

In Italy, from the Brenner to Rome, from the King down to the peasants, the Duce receives welcomes such as I have never seen. He says himself that this enthusiasm was only equalled on the evening when the Empire was proclaimed.

Ribbentrop has handed me a project for a tripartite alliance between Italy, Germany, and Japan. He says it is 'the biggest thing in the world'. He always exaggerates, Ribbentrop. No doubt we will study it quite calmly and, perhaps, put it aside for some time.

[1] André François-Poncet, French Ambassador in Berlin. Ambassador in Rome, November 1938. French High Commissioner in Germany, 1949.

From *Ciano's Diary* translated by A Mayor.

Questions
1 According to Ciano, how did the Munich conference originate?
2 What impressions does he give of the British Ambassador, Lord Perth?
3 Are the reasons attributed to Hitler by Ciano for attacking Czechoslovakia consistent with those reasons given to Chamberlain at Berchtesgaden and Godesberg (Sources 20 and 21) and to the German people at the Sportpalast (Source 22).
4 What does this source convey about the atmosphere of the conference?
5 According to Ciano, who did Daladier blame for the situation?
6 What impression does Ciano give of the Italians' role in the conference? What impression does he create of Mussolini and himself in his diary? How reliable a source do you think his diary is?

This is taken from the editorial of September 30 in the *Glasgow Herald* suggesting what the likely outcome of the talks at Munich will be.

1914 - 1938

The Chief Ministers of four Great Powers have been in Munich together for less than a day, and it seems that they have already succeeded in making an agreement which will prevent a war that seemed almost inevitable 24 hours before they came together. The precise merits of this agreement's details we cannot know as yet. It may appear to promise a sure foundation for settled conditions in Central Europe or it may have in it the seeds of future disputes. But the achievement of present peace seems incontestable, and it is equally incontestable that in the eyes of the democratic peoples at least, the main credit for this achievement will go to one man, the PRIME MINISTER of Great Britain. Others have helped to make the Munich meeting possible – President ROOSEVELT, whose very pointed appeals must have had their effect on Herr HITLER; Signor MUSSOLINI, who seems to have grasped eagerly and promptly a suggestion made to him through the BRITISH AMBASSADOR in Rome; and (one must add) the British Navy and French Army, whose evident preparedness provided the sharpest of arguments in favour of a "peace conference before the war." But it is above all Mr CHAMBERLAIN who has succeeded in doing now what Sir EDWARD GREY vainly wished to do 24 years ago. It is a success which whatever its final results, must mark a new epoch in European affairs and give its author a notable place in history.

This Munich conference is, indeed, the final proof of a change in the nature of war and of international politics. One cannot blame the statesmen of 1914 because they were unable to do what has been done now. They were faced with circumstances which made action of the kind which Mr CHAMBERLAIN has taken during the last few weeks very nearly impossible. In a dozen ways their world was controlled, far more firmly than ours is, by precedents and programmes. These were, in the first place, the military programmes. When the international crisis of 24 years ago reached its height the great armies of the continent began, almost simultaneously to mobilise. Each moved to a timetable, and every Power feared to hold up the movement of its own forces, even for a day, lest its enemies might fail to do likewise and so be in a position to strike first. In 1938, Germany was, for all practical purposes, mobilised before the crisis was fully developed. But France, protected by her Maginot Line and Russia, lying beyond the eastern frontiers of Poland, have felt themselves in no immediate danger of invasion, while the Czechs have also been able, with admirable courage, to stand unmoved behind their own defences.

And there have been other changes. Rather psychological than directly military. Europe no longer thinks in terms of land warfare alone. Every nation is now only too well aware that a great many of its civilians may find themselves in the firing line, so that efforts for peace have a new urgency behind them. And 20 years of the League of Nations have accustomed us to see heads of governments and Foreign Ministers flying across Europe to discuss international affairs with the leaders of other states. In 1914 the conventions of diplomacy were themselves too rigid to have allowed Mr ASQUITH or Sir EDWARD GREY to set off at an hour's notice, for Berlin. A fortnight ago the world might be startled by Mr CHAMBERLAIN's flight to Berchtesgaden, but it could understand that such a visit need not be a mere surrender to the threat of force.

Mr CHAMBERLAIN's achievement has sprung from a simple common sense which allowed him to realise more clearly than most contemporary statesmen what this new freedom of movement and action could mean in a moment of crisis. The new age in European affairs which his patiently repeated efforts helped to reveal to us is unlikely to be any Utopia of peace and mutual understanding. Its dangers may be as real and menacing as those of the past. There may be peril in the recasting of international conventions; certainly there are forces in the totalitarian States of today which will be tamed only with difficulty. But the nations are in one sense at least drawn closer together by the conditions which have permitted the conference at Munich. And if there are new possibilities of trouble ahead of us there are also new hopes of international cooperation.

From *The Glasgow Herald* September 30, 1938.

Questions
1 Does the *Herald* approve of Chamberlain's actions? Support your answer by using evidence from the passage.
2 How does it explain Hitler's decision to come to the conference table?
3 Which of the reasons given do you think was most influential in getting Hitler to the conference table?
4 What had Chamberlain succeeded in doing which "Sir Edward Gray (had) vainly wished to do 24 years ago"?
5 What changes does the *Herald* note in European diplomacy?

Winston Churchhill had opposed appeasement right from the start. *Hansard* records this most potent of speakers at full power in the post-Munich debate in the Commons.

Mr Churchill: I will begin by saying what everybody would like to ignore or forget but which must nevertheless be stated namely, that we have sustained a total and unmitigated defeat, and that France has suffered even more than we have.

Viscountess Astor: Nonsense

Mr Churchill: When the Noble Lady cries "Nonsense," she could not have heard the Chancellor of the Exchequer admit in his illuminating and comprehensive speech just now that Herr Hitler had gained in this particular leap forward in substance all he set out to gain. The utmost my right honourable Friend the Prime Minister has been able to secure by all his immense exertions, by all the great efforts and mobilisation which took place in this country, and by all the anguish and strain through which we have passed in this country, the utmost he has been able to gain - [Hon. Members: "Is peace"] I thought I might be allowed to make that point in its due place, and I propose to deal with it. The utmost he has been able to gain for Czechoslovakia and in the matters which were in dispute has been that the German dictator, instead of snatching his victuals from the table, has been content to have them served to him course by course.

The Chancellor of the Exchequer said it was the first time Herr Hitler had been made to retract - I think that was the word - in any degree. We really must not waste time, after all this long Debate, upon the difference between the positions reached at Berchtesgaden, at Godesberg and at Munich. They can be very simply epitomised, if the House will permit me to vary the metaphor. £1 was demanded at the pistol's point. When it was given, £2 were demanded at the pistol's point. Finally the dictator consented to take £1 17s 6d and the rest in promises of good will for the future.

Now I come to the point, which was mentioned to me just now from some quarters of the House, about the saving of the peace. No one has been a more resolute and uncompromising struggler for peace than the Prime Minister. Everyone knows that. Never has there been such intense and undaunted determination to maintain and to secure peace. That is quite true. Nevertheless, I am not quite clear why there was so much danger of Great Britain or France being in a war with Germany at this juncture if, in fact, they were ready all along to sacrifice Czechoslovakia. The terms which the Prime Minister brought back with him - I quite agree at the last moment: everything had got off the rails and nothing but his intervention could have saved the peace, but I am talking of the events of the summer - could easily have been agreed, I believe, through the ordinary diplomatic channels at any time during the summer ....

All is over. Silent, mournful, abandoned, broken, Czechoslovakia recedes into the darkness. She has suffered in every respect by her association with the Western democracies and with the League of Nations of which she has always been an obedient servant. She has suffered in particular from her association with France, under whose guidance and policy she has been actuated for so long.

I venture to think that in future the Czechoslovak State cannot be maintained as an independent entity. You will find that in a period of time which may be measured by years, but may be measured only by months, Czechoslovakia will be engulfed in the Nazi régime .... But we cannot consider the abandonment and ruin of Czechoslovakia in the light only of what happened only last month. It is the most grievous consequence which we have yet experienced of what we have done and of what we have left undone in the last five years of eager search for the line of least resistance, five years of uninterrupted retreat of British power, five years of neglect of our air defences. Those are the features which I stand here to declare and which marked an improvident stewardship for which Great Britain and France have dearly to pay. We have been reduced in those five years from a position of security so overwhelming and so unchallengeable that we never cared to think about it. We have been reduced from a position where the very word 'war' was considered one which would be used only by persons qualifying for a lunatic asylum. We have been reduced from a position of safety and power - power to do good, power to be generous to a beaten foe, power to make terms with Germany, power to give her proper redress for her grievances, power to stop her arming if we chose, power to take any step in strength or mercy or justice which we thought right - reduced in five years from a position safe and unchallenged to where we stand now.

When I think of the fair hopes of a long peace which still lay before Europe at the beginning of 1933 when Herr Hitler first obtained power, and of all the opportunities of arresting the growth of the Nazi power which have been thrown away, when I think of the immense combinations and resources which have been neglected or squandered, I cannot believe that a parallel exists in the whole course of history. So far as this country is concerned the responsibility must rest with those who have the undisputed control of our political affairs. They neither prevented Germany from rearming, nor did they rearm ourselves in time. They quarrelled with Italy without saving Ethiopia. They exploited and discredited the vast institution of the League of Nations and they neglected to make alliances and combinations which might have repaired previous errors, and thus they left us in the hour of trial without adequate national defence or effective international security....

You have to consider the character of the Nazi movement and the rule which it implies .... there can never be friendship between the British democracy and the Nazi Power, that Power which spurns Christian ethics, which cheers its onward course by a barbarous paganism, which vaunts the spirit of aggression and conquest, which derives strength and perverted pleasure from persecution, and uses, as we have seen, with pitiless brutality the threat of murderous force. That Power cannot ever be the trusted friend of the British democracy.

What I find unendurable is the sense of our country falling into the power, into the orbit and influence of Nazi Germany, and of our existence becoming dependent upon their good will or pleasure. It is to prevent that I have tried my best to urge the maintenance of every bulwark of defence - first the timely creation of an Air Force superior to anything within striking distance of our shores; secondly, the gathering together of the collective strength of many nations; and thirdly, the making of alliances and military conventions, all within the Covenant, in order to gather together forces at any rate to restain the onward movement of this Power.

It has all been in vain. Every position has been successively undermined and abandoned on specious and plausible excuses. We do not want to be led upon the high road to becoming a satellite of the German Nazi system of European domination. In a very few years, perhaps in a very few months, we shall be confronted with demands with which we shall no doubt be invited to comply. Those demands may affect the surrender of territory or the surrender of liberty. I foresee and foretell that the policy of submission will carry with it restrictions upon the freedom of speech and debate in Parliament, on public platforms, and discussions in the Press, for it will be said - indeed, I hear it said sometimes now - that we cannot allow the Nazi system of dictatorship to be criticised by ordinary common English politicians. Then, with a Press under control, in part direct but more potently indirect, with every organ of public opinion doped and chloroformed into acquiescence, we shall be conducted along further stages of our journey ....

I do not grudge our loyal, brave people, who were ready to do their duty no matter what the cost, who never flinched under the strain of last week - I do not grudge them the natural, spontaneous outburst of joy and relief when they learned that the hard ordeal would no longer be required of them at the moment; but they should know the truth. They should know that there has been gross neglect and deficiency in our defences; they should know that we have sustained a defeat without a war, the consequences of which will travel far with us along our road; they should know that we have passed an awful milestone in our history, when the whole equilibrium of Europe has been deranged, and that the terrible words have for the time being been pronounced against the Western democracies:

"Thou art weighed in the balance and found wanting"

And do not suppose that this is the end. This is only the beginning of the reckoning. This is only the first sip, the first foretaste of a bitter cup which will be proffered to us year by year unless by a supreme recovery of moral health and martial vigour, we arise again and take our stand for freedom as in the olden time.

Hansard 5 October 1938

Following Hitler's betrayal of his promises to permit the survival of the Czech State, made at the Munich Conference, Chamberlain spoke in the House of Commons about Poland. Many believed that Poland would be Hitler's next target.

Source 26

The right honourable Gentleman, the Leader of the Opposition, asked me this morning whether I could make a statement as to the European situation. As I said this morning, His Majesty's Government have no official confirmation of the rumours of any projected attack on Poland and they must not, therefore, be taken as accepting them as true.

I am glad to take this opportunity of stating again the general policy of His Majesty's Government. They have constantly advocated the adjustment, by way of free negotiation between the parties concerned, of any differences that may arise between them. They consider that this is the natural and proper course where differences exist. In their opinion there should be no question incapable of solution by peaceful means, and they would see no justification for the substitution of force or threats of force for the method of

As the house is aware, certain consultations are now proceeding with other Governments. In order to make perfectly clear the position of His Majesty's Government in the meantime before those consultations are concluded, I now have to inform the House that during that period, in the event of any action which clearly threatened Polish independence, and which the Polish Government accordingly considered it vital to resist with their national forces, His Majesty's Government would feel themselves bound at once to lend the Polish Government all support in their power. They have given the Polish Government an assurance to this effect.

I may add that the French Government have authorised me to make it plain that they stand in the same position in this matter as do His Majesty's Government.

(From *Hansard*, 31 March 1939)

Questions
1 How does Churchill's view differ from the *Herald's* view in Source 24? Select any two examples from the extract to support your answer.
2 What did Churchill mean by "I am not quite clear why there was so much danger of Great Britain and France being in a war with Germany ... if ... they were ready all along to sacrifice Czechoslovakia."?
3 What does Churchill predict will happen to Czechoslovakia?
4 What does he see as the Government's main failings in the period 1933-38?
5 Explain why Churchill thought that there could never be friendly relations between Britain and Nazi Germany.
6 What do you understand by Churchill's phrase "This is only the beginning of the reckoning."?
7 How effective do you consider Churchill's speech was in putting across the message that the Munich Agreement was a "total and unmitigated defeat for Britain"?

Questions
1 How would Chamberlain ideally have liked the Polish question to be settled?
2 What help did he propose to offer Poland?
3 In what way did the offer of help indicate a significant change in British foreign policy?
4 Why do you think Chamberlain was now willing to give Poland assurances?
5 In your opinion, was this a correct move by Chamberlain? Give evidence to support your answer.

BIBLIOGRAPHY

The books and documents listed below are the principal sources of the information contained in this book. The asterisks are not an attempt to comment on the overall merit of the books; they merely indicate which ones would make appropriate further reading for a student working for the SCE revised Higher History exam.

GENERAL TEXTS COVERING THE WHOLE TOPIC

* EH Carr International Relations between the Wars [MacMillan]
* Martin Gilbert Britain and Germany between the Wars[Longmans]
* GM Gathorne-Hardy A Short History of International Relations. 1920-1939 [OUP]
Gordon Martel Origins of the Second World War Reconsidered [Allen and Unwin]
Russell Stone The Drift to War [Heinemann]
* FP Walters The League of Nations [OUP]
* Robert Wolfson Years of Change [Arnold]

BACKGROUND

Keith Feiling Neville Chamberlain [MacMillan 1946]
* Martin Gilbert The Roots of Appeasement [Plume Books]
A Lentin Guilt at Versailles. The Pre-history of Appeasement [Methuen]
* Keith Robbins Appeasement [Blackwell]

ABYSSINIA

* AJ Barker The Rape of Ethiopia. Purnell's History of the 20th Century, Chapter 57. [1969]
Ethiopia, Unclaimed Colony same publication.
*Richard Collier Duce! The Rise and Fall of Benito Mussolini
Anthony Mockler Haile Selassie's War [Grafton Books].

SPAIN

* Harry Browne Spain's Civil War [Longmans]
Michael Foot Aneurin Bevan - Vol. 1 [Four Square]
* Ernest Hemingway For Whom the Bell Tolls [Penguin]
* Peter Kemp Mine Were of Trouble [Cassell]
*Ian MacDougall Voices from the Spanish Civil War [Polygon]
* George Orwell Homage to Catalonia [Penguin]
* Robert Payne The Civil War in Spain 1936-1939 [Secker & Warburg].
* LE Snellgrove Franco and the Spanish Civil War [Longmans]
* Hugh Thomas The Spanish Civil War [Pelican]
* Strathclyde Regional Council Education Department Perspectives on the Spanish Civil War (Resources Pack)

GERMANY AND GERMAN FOREIGN POLICY

* Alan Bullock Hitler, a study in Tyranny [Pelican]
* William Carr Arms, Autarky and Aggression. A study in German Foreign Policy 1933-1939 [Arnold]

Fritz Fischer From Kaiserreich to Third Reich [Allen & Unwin]
Martin Gilbert Britain and Germany between the Wars [Longman]
* Ruth Henig Origins of the Second World War [Methuen]
Klaus Hildebrand The Foreign Policy of the Third Reich [Batsford]
AJP Taylor Origins of the Second World War [Penguin]
* DG Williamson The Third Reich [Longmans]

PRIMARY SOURCES AND COLLECTIONS OF DOCUMENTS

* Anthony Adamthwaite The Making of the Second World War [Allen and Unwin]
* Anthony Adamthwaite The Lost Peace [Arnold]
Norman H Baynes The Speeches of Adolf Hitler [OUP]
Ciano's Diary 1937-1938 translated by A Mayor [Methuen & Co.]
A Duff Cooper Old Men Forget [Rupert Hart Davies]
Documents in British Foreign Policy 1919-39 ed. Medlicott and Dakin [HMSO]
 Second Series Vol.XIV (deals with Abyssinia and the Rhineland)
Documents in German Foreign Policy [HMSO]
 Series C Vol.V (deals with the Rhineland / 1936)
 Series D Vol.I (deals with Austria and the Anschluss)
 Series D Vol.II (deals with the Czech crisis)
 Series D Vol.III (deals with the Spanish Civil War)
Adolf Hitler Mein Kampf translated by R Mannheim [Hutchinson]
Hitler's 'Secret Book' [Evergreen Books]
League of Nations Geneva 1932, Report of the Lytton Commission
Viscount Templewood (Sir S Hoare) Nine Troubled Years [Collins]

OTHER USEFUL MATERIAL

BBC Schools TV Advanced Level History Programme on Munich.
BBC Schools TV Twentieth Century History Programme Why Appeasement?
Channel 4 Video The World at War Programmes 1 & 2 Czechoslovakia and Poland.
Channel 4 Video No Easy Road Programme 1 Ethiopia's Independence
Trax Videos (Between the Wars) No.6 The Abyssinian Crisis & The Spanish Civil War

INDEX